D0449911

Presented To:

_____

From:

_____

Date:

_____

STRENGTH
— to —
STAND

BOOKS BY T.D. JAKES

40 Days of Power

Anointing Fall on Me

Can You Stand to Be Blessed?

Help Me, I've Fallen and I Can't Get Up!

Hope for Every Moment

Naked and Not Ashamed

Power for Living

Release Your Anointing

Release Your Destiny, Release Your Anointing

The Harvest

Water in the Wilderness

Why? Because You Are Anointed

Wisdom from T.D. Jakes

Woman, Thou Art Loosed

AVAILABLE FROM DESTINY IMAGE PUBLISHERS

STRENGTH
— to —
STAND

**Overcoming, Succeeding,
Thriving, Advancing, Winning!**

T.D. JAKES

DESTINY IMAGE® PUBLISHERS, INC.
P.O. Box 310, Shippensburg, PA 17257-0310

"Promoting Inspired Lives"

This book and all other Destiny Image, Revival Press, MercyPlace,
Fresh Bread, Destiny Image Fiction, and Treasure House books are
available at Christian bookstores and distributors worldwide.

For a U.S. bookstore nearest you, call 1-800-722-6774.
For more information on foreign distributors, call 717-532-3040.
Reach us on the Internet: www.destinyimage.com.

ISBN 13 TP: 978-0-7684-3876-5
ISBN 13 Ebook: 978-0-7684-8965-1
ISBN 13 Hardcover: 978-0-7684-3877-2

For Worldwide Distribution, Printed in the U.S.A.
1 2 3 4 5 6 7 8 9 10 11 / 13 12 11

Contents

Foreword

I cannot think of a greater living example of the consistent ability to draw on the *strength to stand* through the anointing of the Lord. T.D. Jakes is a man without equal. There is much we can all learn from his words, his spirit, and his passion in delivering the word of the Lord. Just watching him is a wonder in itself. The presence of the Lord flows freely from him as he teaches. He is simple, clear, and honest in his delivery; sometimes urgent, sometimes gentle, but always accurate and penetrating. He is a man whose inner focus is on the Lord Himself. Even in his most emotional presentation, you can also see the rest and peace in his eyes.

The strength and power of the Holy Spirit will always move freely through those who have no other desire than to share the word of the Lord to hungry people. And make no mistake about it, God has much to say to His people. He has much He wants to communicate to the world around us. There is much to learn from the Bishop's words, but also his method, his passion, and his love of the Lord Jesus.

I first met the Bishop at a small conference in the Pocono Mountains where he was ministering. That was just before he wrote *Woman, Thou Art Loosed*. We literally walked into each other that fateful afternoon in the basement area of the conference center where vendors were displaying their products. The moment I touched him I prophesied about a book churning in his heart. A few weeks later he called me and the rest, as they say, is history.

There are three criteria we use when determining the possibility of publishing a new author. We look at the person, his message, and his ministry. In the Bishop's case, all three were intricately wrapped with integrity, gentleness, and truth. We are proud to offer this work to you. He is a man who has allowed the Lord to mold him into a vessel He can use to change the lives of millions around the world. We are grateful to be part of God's plan for the life of Bishop T.D. Jakes.

Don Nori Sr.
Founder
Destiny Image Publishers

Introduction

This book will equip you to meet the devil's end-time onslaught to thwart the plan of God. Believers are equipped with the *Strength to Stand* because of the anointing of the Holy Spirit. Whether or not we make ourselves available to that strength is the question.

You are capable of achieving more than you ever imagined by accessing the power that the Lord God has designed especially for you. His master plan is to carry you to new and exciting heights of splendor, hope, and love.

When economic troubles, family struggles, political upheavals, and natural disasters take center stage, you can rest assured with an inner peace that passes all understanding, that you have the power to victoriously live through it all. You are the salt of the earth, the beacon in a dark world, the refreshing stream for a thirsty land.

Only through the powerful anointing of the Holy Spirit will the Church forge ahead with strength to overcome, succeed, thrive, advance, and win! As we share our Savior with others, His best flows through us to make the world a safer, stronger, and more beautiful place. A place where children are welcomed, and grandparents are respected; a place where Jesus is Lord and His Kingdom will come.

The strength to stand through whatever comes your way is at your fingertips. As you discover His will for you, keep your heart, mind, and spirit open to receive His anointing. Allow Him to fill you to overflowing, and watch your family, coworkers, and those around you enjoy the glory of God splashing all over them!

Christians must know that their lives with God can be full of new experiences every day. Instead of merely enduring our salvation, we can enjoy the fullness that God has provided in the Holy Spirit—by availing ourselves to His strength and power within us.

If you have been saved by the grace of God, you have a calling on your life. God may want you to be a pastor, an evangelist, or a missionary. He may call you to be a light in the business world. You may have been apprehended by the hand of God to write books, lead people in worship, or raise godly children.

These gifts and callings were not placed in your life to lie dormant. Only by the power of the Holy Ghost will you see them fulfilled. This book shows you how to meet challenges and overcome them victoriously as you have the strength to stand and to realize your full potential.

If you apply these practical truths in your life, you will begin to experience a new freshness in God. The plans that you have hoped to fulfill all your life will become reality. Do you long for certain things in God? Does your sanctified soul stir at the thought of doing exploits for God? A sense of destiny causes you to determine, "No matter what I must go through, I can and will make it!" These truths will take you to higher heights and deeper depths in God.

Get ready to experience a new joy and strength that will change your life as you overcome adversity, succeed in achieving your goals, thrive in all aspects of your life, advance your dreams and visions, and win each race that you run with the grace of God.

CHAPTER 1

Your Strength to Stand

*Who are you to judge another's servant? To his own master he stands or falls. Indeed, he will be made to stand, for **God is able to make him** [you] **stand*** (Romans 14:4).

Do you believe God is able to pick you up and make you stand? Until you know that God is able, you will never cry out for His help.

God asked the prophet Isaiah, *"Hast thou not known? hast thou not heard, that the everlasting God, the LORD, the Creator of the ends of the earth, fainteth not, neither is weary?"* (Isa. 40:28a KJV).

God wants us to understand that there is no lack of strength in Him. You may not have much of a prayer life, but God says, "Has thou not known?" In other words, you should have known that He would take care of you.

The Word says that the everlasting God, the Creator of the universe, is all powerful. He has brought you through many problems, so don't let satan deceive you into thinking that it was just luck or coincidence that delivered you.

God is my strength and my power, and He makes my way perfect (2 Samuel 22:33).

Remember what God has done for you. If you can't seem to remember anything He has done for you personally, then look around at others who have been delivered out of situations worse than yours. See what God did for them and tell yourself, "If He can do it for them, I know He can do it for me."

God's divine love and power brought them through, and He will do the same for you. God says, "I have the strength that is necessary to escalate and motivate and move you up and out of your circumstances."

REMEMBER WHAT GOD HAS DONE FOR YOU.

Some live in rebellion against God's Word, which clearly commands:

Trust in the LORD with all thine heart; and lean not unto thine own understanding. In all thy ways acknowledge Him, and He shall direct thy paths (Proverbs 3:5-6 KJV).

Because of their pride, such people never seek God's counsel on anything or consult the advice of the Word of God on important decisions. When they do go to the Bible about some matter or pressing issue, they misinterpret God's Word to make it mean what they want it to say. They have become very skilled and crafty at erroneously using the Word to rationalize and justify their own selfish motivations.

Remember, *"There is a way which seemeth right unto a man, but the end thereof are the ways of death"* (Prov. 14:12 KJV).

Instead of traveling this road of destruction, you can take the righteous alternative, which is the counsel of God. If you want to be victorious in all your endeavors, then don't lean on your own understanding or to your own devices or innovations. Instead, in all your ways acknowledge the Lord, and He will direct your path.

Trust in the LORD *with all your heart, and lean not on your own understanding; in all your ways acknowledge Him, and He shall direct your paths* (Proverbs 3:5-6).

Seek the Word of the Lord about everything that concerns you, and you will, like the great warrior Joshua, have good success.

If you want to be profitable in business and successful in life, develop an attitude and habit of inquiring of the Lord, and you will never fail. Turn from the wicked way of your own fleshly wisdom and acknowledge the Lord—and He will direct your path.

For as many as are led by the Spirit of God, these are sons of God (Romans 8:14).

Renewed Strength

The Bible says that God, *"gives power to the weak, and to those who have no might He increases strength"* (Isa. 40:29). In other words, He is saying, "I won't kill you because you fainted. I give power to the weak."

When you start losing the strength you once had, you are fainting. When you can hardly stand up, and you begin to stagger in the throes of sin, lust, envy, and strife, God declares, "I give power to the weak [faint]!"

God says, "I give power, not to the person who is standing strong, but to the one who is swaying on wobbly knees. I give power to the faint." To those who have no might, He said, "I will increase their strength."

If you have looked inside yourself and cannot muster the strength to get up, God says, "I will increase your strength."

Think back for a moment to the elderly woman in that television commercial when she said, "Help, I've fallen and I can't get up." She did not only need someone to help her up, but she needed someone or something to make her stronger.

God will not only raise you up, but He'll give you enough power to pull yourself up if you stumble again. He won't help you up so you can be handicapped the rest of your life. No. He gives power to the faint, and to those who are weak He gives strength.

GOD GIVES POWER TO THE WEAK.

Are you weak with no will-power, no strength, no ability within yourself to resist the enemy? When your body gets tired, remember God and His strength. When satan begins to attack you, remember the power of God residing within your innermost being. Remember that God does not faint or grow weary. In fact, the Holy One does not even sleep.

*Create in me a clean heart, O God, and renew a steadfast **spirit within me*** (Psalm 51:10).

When you remember these things about your Father, your strength will suddenly be renewed. Your joy will be restored, and your power will return. You will begin to experience a life of victory.

Waiting on God

God says, "If you wait on Me, I'll renew your strength. If you wait on Me, everything will be all right."

*But those who wait on the LORD shall **renew their strength;** they shall mount up with wings like eagles, they shall run and not be weary, they shall walk and not faint* (Isaiah 40:31).

You may be hurt right now, but be patient. Help is on the way.

I know you've cried out, "Lord, help! I've fallen, and I can't get up." The Holy Spirit says, "Wait. Help is on the way. Just hold on, God is coming to your aid. He's coming to deliver you and to set you free."

God is going to bring you out and loose you from your captivity. He's going to renew your strength. If you hold on a little while longer, your change is going to come.

Remember Samson who lost everything; he lost his hair, his strength, and his eyes. Samson lost his position, his family, his wife, and his reputation. He was reduced from a great warrior to grinding at the mill. But without a doubt, at an appointed time, Samson's strength was renewed.

Samson's attitude was, "Lord, I'm waiting on You. If You don't help me, I'll die without ever being redeemed from the error of my ways. Lord, if You don't help me, I'll never get my honor back. God, if You don't help me, I'll never get up from where I've fallen."

While he was waiting, Samson's strength began to return.

The secret to renewing your strength is waiting on the Lord. God's Word says, *"But they that wait upon the LORD shall renew their strength…"* (Isa. 40:31 KJV).

At times you may not have been able to explain it or prove it, but you knew you were waiting on something to happen in your life. The devil said, "You need to give up and die," but something inside you said, "Hold out a little while longer."

The devil said, "You're not going to get it," but something else said, "Wait. You're hurting, but wait; you're crying, but wait; you've missed it, but wait on the Lord and everything is going to be all right."

On Eagles' Wings

...they shall mount up on wings like eagles, they shall run and not be weary, they shall walk and not faint (Isaiah 40:31).

God declares, "I'll cause your wings to stretch out. You will mount up on wings like eagles. I'll take you above the top of the storm clouds."

The eagle does not fly in the storm; it flies *above* the storm. Spreading its wings wide, the eagle uses the wind blowing against it to take it higher instead of lower.

You don't have to let the wind bring you down. If you just stretch out on God's Word, the same wind that is trying to take you under will hold you up and take you over into the glory of God.

You're going to walk and not faint, but first you must come to God with your whole heart. Humble yourself and tell the Lord that you're unable to do it alone. Tell the Lord that you've tried, but you can't seem to get the victory—you just can't get up.

"Lord, I've been lying here on the ground of adversity and defeat. I've tried, but I can't get up. The desire is there in my mind and my will, but when I try to get back on my feet, I can't get my flesh to cooperate with what the Word of God says I can do. I'm thinking right, but I'm not doing right. I'm saying the right things, but I can't get up."

"LORD, HELP ME!"

It is at this point that you must call out: "Lord, You've got to help me, or I'll never get out of this. Lord, help! I've fallen, and I can't get up! I'm pretending to be stronger than I am, but I need You to renew my strength. God, give me back my will to fight."

> *Then Samson called to the LORD, saying, "**O Lord GOD,** remember me, I pray! **Strengthen me,** I pray, just this once, O God...* (Judges 16:28).

You also need to confess: "Lord, I know I'm allowing things in my life that should not be there. I repent of my sin. I want to be delivered, but I continue to be bound. I don't have the strength to deliver myself. I need the Holy Spirit working in my life again."

Brothers and sisters, when your situation gets desperate, you need to run to God like you have never run before and cry out: "Jesus, I'm on the verge of destruction. If You don't help me, the enemy is going to annihilate me. He's about to take me out! Help me, Lord Jesus!"

The Holy Spirit is calling you. Put away the excuses and the complaints. God is calling you. Give Him everything, and allow Him to renew your strength.

> *Now David was greatly distressed, for the people spoke of stoning him, because the soul of all the people was grieved, every man for his sons and his daughters. But David* ***strengthened himself in the LORD*** *his God* (1 Samuel 30:6).

The areas of your life that you have not given up to Him, you need to release right now. Don't be bound any longer. The Lord will not renew your strength until you are willing to throw everything on the altar, without restrictions or reservations.

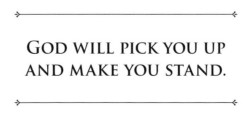

GOD WILL PICK YOU UP
AND MAKE YOU STAND.

When you've given Him all of you, He'll give you all of Him—no more "some" of you and "some" of Him. It's time in your life that it's "none" of you and "all" of Him.

*And to love Him with **all** the heart, with **all** the under-standing, with **all** the soul, and with **all** the strength...* (Mark 12:33).

When you make that decision, He'll enable you to mount up on eagles' wings and soar with the mighty wind of the Spirit.

God will pick you up and make you stand.

Stamina Secrets and Solutions

1. Do you believe God is able to pick you up and make you stand? List the things and/or people keeping you from standing. Are these things/people greater than the God you serve?

   _____

   _____

   _____

   _____

2. Until you know that God is able, you will never cry out for His help. When is the last time you cried out for Him? Did He come to your rescue?

   _____

   _____

   _____

   _____

3. Have you ever heard the devil say, "You need to give up and die"? What was your response to him? Do you believe the devil over what God tells you?

   _____

   _____

   _____

   _____

4. When you felt like giving up, did you hear a still, small voice telling you to, "Hold out a little while longer"? Did you give up or did you obey the Holy Spirit's voice?

_____

_____

_____

_____

5. The Lord will not renew your strength until you are willing to throw everything on the altar, without restrictions or reservations. How badly do you want strength and power to overcome what you're going through? Enough to go to the altar with your life in your hands?

_____

_____

_____

_____

CHAPTER 2

Who Is Your God?

Jesus answered and said to him, "…For it is
written, 'You shall worship the LORD your God,
and Him only you shall serve'" (Luke 4:8).

My God is the Alpha and the Omega, the Beginning and the End. There is nothing too hard for Him. There is nothing He cannot handle.

Because we know who we are in Christ Jesus and what we mean to our heavenly Father, satan tries to discourage us. He tries to use sickness, financial problems, family stress, and anything and everything you can think of to incapacitate us. The questions you must ask yourself: "Who is my God? Whom do I serve?" must be answered with, "My God is the Way-Maker."

The Bible says that if God be for us, who can be against us?

*What then shall we say to these things? If **God is for us,** who can be against us?* (Romans 8:31)

God is so real in my inward man. He has not only washed away all my sins, but He has filled my cup with His love so that my cup bubbles over. He is the Lover of my soul; He is the Answer to my every need; He is my Burden-Bearer. Maybe you are the kind of person who can handle everything that comes your way, but I can't. However, I know Someone who is able to take it. His name is Jesus Christ.

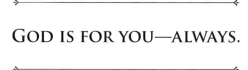

GOD IS FOR YOU—ALWAYS.

The enemy fights those who know who they are and whose they are. The Bible affirms that God is faithful: *"God is faithful, by whom you were called into the fellowship of His Son, Jesus Christ our Lord"* (1 Cor. 1:9). The Word of God also states:

> *Yet for us there is* **one God,** *the Father, of whom are all things, and we for Him; and* **one Lord Jesus Christ,** *through whom are all things, and through whom we live* (1 Corinthians 8:6).

Are you aware that the more the enemy fights you, the greater the indication that blessings are on the way? You must be cognizant of this fact as a Christian. If you do not know that about life, you cannot make it. You have got to know that it is because you are on the verge of a miracle that the devil is fighting you. He is fighting you so hard because you are getting closer to your deliverance; and the closer you get, the greater the struggle.

> *Be sober, be vigilant; because your adversary the devil walks about like a roaring lion, seeking whom he may devour* (1 Peter 5:8).

If you hold out a little while longer, God's going to give you the victory in every circumstance of your life. I am learning to be encouraged when I meet with obstacles because I see them as an indication of a fresh move of God in my life.

When people ask you who your God is, how do you respond? With confidence, your shoulders held high, and a smile on your face you can say, "He is everything I will ever need. He is my Father, the Creator of Heaven and earth, and the One who sustains the universe. He is Jehovah, the I AM that I AM."

> *And God said to Moses, "I AM WHO I AM." And He said, "Thus you shall say to the children of Israel, 'I AM has sent me to you'"* (Exodus 3:14).

God's Got a Plan

When you are in the wilderness, you must find out what the plan of God is for you. You cannot rely on anyone else's plan. Only a plan from God will suffice in the wilderness.

God has not promised that you will not go through hardship, neither has He promised that you will not experience adversity. But listen to what He says: "When you pass through the waters, I will be with you. When you go through the flood, I'll be there. Should you have to go through fire, I will be there. As I was with Shadrach, Meshach, and Abednego, so will I be with you. I will be the fourth One in the furnace."

> *And these three men, Shadrach, Meshach, and Abed-Nego, fell down bound into the midst of the burning fiery furnace. Then King Nebuchadnezzar was astonished; and he rose in haste and spoke, saying to his counselors, "Did we not cast three men bound into the midst of the fire?" They answered and said to the king, "True, O king." "Look!" he answered,* **"I see four men loose, walking in the midst of the fire; and they are not hurt, and the form of the fourth is like the Son of God."** *Then Nebuchadnezzar went near the mouth of the burning fiery furnace and spoke, saying, "Shadrach,*

Meshach, and Abed-Nego, servants of the Most High God, come out, and come here." Then Shadrach, Meshach, and Abed-Nego came from the midst of the fire.

*And the satraps, administrators, governors, and the king's counselors gathered together, and they saw these men on whose bodies **the fire had no power**; the hair of their head was not singed nor were their garments affected, and the smell of fire was not on them. Nebuchadnezzar spoke, saying, **"Blessed be the God of Shadrach, Meshach, and Abed-Nego, who sent His Angel and delivered His servants who trusted in Him,** and they have frustrated the king's word, and yielded their bodies, that they should not serve nor worship any god except their own God! Therefore I make a decree that any people, nation, or language which speaks anything amiss against the God of Shadrach, Meshach, and Abed-Nego shall be cut in pieces, and their houses shall be made an ash heap; because **there is no other God who can deliver like this"** (Daniel 3:23-29).*

I am very grateful that the Lord's been walking with me all these years. I say this not because I have not been through anything, or that I have not faced various challenges and dark moments in life, but I do recognize that the Lord has been the fourth One in the fiery furnace. He has protected me from the scorching of the flames. When the pressure and the flames seemed as if they would engulf me, His words of assurance would comfort me.

There are many who would have lost their mind had the Lord not been on their side. They would have gone crazy and lost control, but the Lord comforted them in their darkest hour. It is not that we did not go through the wilderness but when we went through it, God was with us. God will be with you when mama, daddy, sister, and brother leave. When the folks you thought would be with you all the way, walk out of the door, God says, *"Lo, I am with you always, even unto the end of the age"* (Matt. 28:20).

"I AM WITH YOU ALWAYS EVEN UNTO THE END OF THE WORLD."

You need not fear the wilderness if you take God with you everywhere you go. I must take Him with me everywhere I go, or else I would fall on my face. I truly need the Lord for I cannot function without Him. I need Him in the morning; I need Him in the noon day; I need Him when the sun is down. I need Him to run my business; I need Him to teach me how to be a good father; I need Him to be a good husband. Don't you try to be anything without God, because you will not succeed.

The enemy may come to discourage you. He may whisper to your mind that God will not help you or that you might have committed a horrible sin that has brought God's wrath on you. Satan thinks that he catches the Lord by surprise. But, oh, is he wrong!

God is a God of plans. He is a God of order. As the God who knows all things, He is never surprised by the attack of the enemy. While the enemy is planning his strategies, God has already made a counter-plan for him. He has already made a way of escape for you. Yes, you must trust Him.

*As for God, His way is perfect; the word of the LORD is proven; He is a shield to all who **trust in Him** (Psalm 18:30).*

*The LORD is good, a stronghold in the day of trouble; and He knows those **who trust in Him** (Nahum 1:7).*

Peter asked the Lord Jesus if he could join Him on the sea. After the Lord told him to come, Peter got out of the boat and walked on the sea until he took his eyes off of Jesus.

*And Peter answered Him and said, "Lord, if it is You,
command me to come to You on the water." So He said,
"Come." And when Peter had come down out of the boat,
he walked on the water to go to Jesus. But when he saw that
the wind was boisterous, he was afraid; and beginning to
sink he cried out, saying, **"Lord, save me!"** And **immediately** Jesus stretched out His hand and caught him…* (Matthew 14:28-31).*

Maybe you are in trouble right now. Maybe you are reading
this book, trying to find answers to your situation. Maybe you
have been trying to run your life without God or you have been
trying to deal with your wilderness without God's help. You may
be convinced you know what you are doing and that you are not
obligated to listen to anyone. Be careful, for pride comes before a
fall. My friend, you do need God. You need Him to help you to
hold your mind together.

You need Him when you are at the breaking point and people
have disappointed you. Nobody else but God will get up with you
at 3:00 A.M. and hold you in His arms. Nobody else but God can
comfort you when you are depressed.

ONLY GOD CAN GIVE YOU PEACE.

Only God can supernaturally soothe your nerves and quell
your worries. Only He can give you that peace that passes all
understanding. When the Scripture talks about the peace that
passes all understanding, it refers to a peace that is anointed.

*Be anxious for nothing, but in everything by prayer and
supplication, with thanksgiving, let your requests be made
known to God; and the **peace of God,** which surpasses all*

understanding, **will guard your hearts and minds** *through Christ Jesus* (Philippians 4:6-7).

When people look at your situation, and then look at you, they will be confused. They will say, "Why is he so peaceful? Doesn't he realize that he has nothing? Everything he had is gone. Why is he so peaceful?" It is simply the God-given peace that you enjoy. Try it. Believe me, you will like it. God says, "It's going to be all right. Just trust Me, just lean on Me, and look to Me for total deliverance."

For I know the thoughts that I think toward you, says the LORD, *thoughts of peace and not of evil, to give you a future and a hope* (Jeremiah 29:11).

You might not be able to see how it will work out, but you've got to trust that before it is all over, God's going to give you the victory.

You see, God's got a plan!

Stamina Secrets and Solutions

1. "My God is the Alpha and the Omega, the Beginning and the End." This may be your conviction too, but what happens in the "middle" of life that takes your heart, spirit, and mind off of God? Commit today to keep focused on God and His unending love for you.

   _____

   _____

   _____

2. God has not only washed away all your sins, but He has filled your cup with His love so that your cup should be bubbling over. What is bubbling out of your cup today? Worship or whining? Praising or pouting? Forgiveness or fretting? It's your choice.

   _____

   _____

   _____

   _____

3. God knows all things; He is never surprised by the attack of the enemy. How surprised are you when the enemy attacks? Do you give in to fear or give fear over to God who will make a way out of the snare for you?

   _____

   _____

   _____

4. Like Peter, if you keep your eyes on Jesus you can conquer every fear. But if you fall, know that Jesus will *immediately* stretch out His arm and catch you. Are you trusting Him today?

_____

_____

_____

5. "Only God can supernaturally soothe your nerves and quell your worries." Are you turning to God, others, drugs, alcohol, Jesus, gambling, pornography, the Holy Spirit, or sex to comfort you? The choices are yours to make daily. Only the Holy Trinity can bring you total peace.

_____

_____

_____

CHAPTER 3

What Comes Before a Fall?

Pride goes before destruction, and a haughty
spirit before a fall (Proverbs 16:18).

Pride comes before a fall. But what is pride? Pride is defined as "being high-minded; showing one's self above others." Another definition states: "Pride is a conceited sense of one's superiority." Pride has caused the fall of many great and gifted individuals.

When Self Is Your God

The first known instance of pride occurred before the creation of the earth. Lucifer, the head angel in charge of praise, decided he was going to be greater than God Himself.

How you are fallen from heaven, O Lucifer, son of the morn-
ing! How you are cut down to the ground, you who weak-
ened the nations! For you have said in your heart: "I will
ascend into heaven, I will exalt my throne above the stars of
God; I will also sit on the mount of the congregation on the

farthest sides of the north; I will ascend above the heights of the clouds, I will be like the Most High" (Isaiah 14:12-14).

Driven by self-deception, prideful self-delusion, and self-importance, lucifer considered himself better than God. This explains why most of his statements begin with the word "I."

Lucifer, whose name at one time meant "light-bearer," was cast down by God to earth, where he would be known as satan. No longer a praise leader or a majestic angel, instead he became one who roams to and fro on the earth like a lion looking for someone to devour.

> *Be sober, be vigilant; because your adversary the devil walks about like a roaring lion, seeking whom he may devour* (1 Peter 5:8).

Satan's pride led to his downfall. Pride and selfishness go hand in hand. Usually where there is pride, there is also the prevailing spirit of selfishness. Selfishness is defined as "loving one's self first."

> *The wicked in his proud countenance does not seek God; God is in none of his thoughts* (Psalm 10:4).

Satan thought he could be better than God Himself. Of course he was wrong. Satan was deceived. How he even conceived such a thought is beyond imagination. But pride blinds us to the truth and prevents the proud from viewing life realistically.

> *For all that is in the world—the lust of the flesh, the lust of the eyes, and the pride of life—is not of the Father but is of the world* (1 John 2:16).

As we know, satan has never repented. Instead, he tries to deceive as many of God's children as possible and drag them down to share in his dreadful fallen state.

A Dangerous Place

The prophet Daniel records the downfall of the great Babylonian king, Nebuchadnezzar. One day, the king looked around at all he had accomplished and arrogantly stated:

Is not this great Babylon, that I have built for a royal dwelling by my mighty power and for the honor of my majesty? (Daniel 4:30).

While he was still speaking these arrogant words, a voice from Heaven said, *"King Nebuchadnezzar, to you it is spoken: the kingdom has departed from you"* (Dan. 4:31). That same hour, the once-great king lost his mind and began to act like an animal, eating grass until *"his hair had grown like eagles' feathers and his nails like birds' claws"* (Dan. 4:33).

Nebuchadnezzar took his eyes off God and began to focus on his accomplishments. Forgetting who had made him great, the king lost touch with reality and denied truth, thinking he was a self-made man who needed no one.

Nebuchadnezzar did not want to give God any of the glory or thanks for the growth and majesty of the kingdom. He felt that everything he owned belonged to him because he had worked for it. Sound familiar?

Pride goes before destruction, and a haughty spirit before a fall (Proverbs 16:18).

When put into a place of prominence, many of God's children forget who brought them to that place. This arrogant and prideful attitude has caused many to fall from the pinnacle of success and popularity.

During the 1980s, several nationally known televangelists let their fame and fortune get the best of them. As a result, pride prevented them from acknowledging their need of God. Considering themselves to be beyond reproach—or advice—they let their guards down. Sin entered their lives, eventually destroying their ministries, their families, and their reputations.

When pride comes, then comes shame; but with the humble is wisdom (Proverbs 11:2).

When people (especially Christians who are not rooted and grounded in the Word) start acquiring prestige and experiencing monetary prosperity, they often forget that not long ago they had nothing. Before they owned a nice new car, they could barely afford to ride the bus. Before they lived in a nice new home, their family of five lived in a two-bedroom apartment, not sure how they were going to pay the rent. They were living from paycheck to paycheck.

In spite of their lack, they still managed to give God the glory whether it was by word of mouth or by giving in the offering. They knew that God would meet their needs. But once they came into a place of prosperity, they forgot it was God and God alone who blessed them. Now they look to their jobs or their businesses—or even their ministries—as their source. That is a dangerous place to be.

Contentment Versus Self-Sufficiency

Where does the slippery slide into delusion begin? With discontent.

Nebuchadnezzar was not content with his increase; he wanted more. The more he was blessed, the more he wanted. His is a clear case of greed and self-sufficiency brought on by self-deception.

Deception is a trap and stronghold that ensnares many, especially those not content with their own present state in life. The Bible instructs us that we must learn to be content in whatever state we find ourselves. The apostle Paul learned that lesson well, *"...for I have learned, in whatsoever state I am, therewith to be content"* (Phil. 4:11 KJV).

This is not to imply that we should be satisfied with being bound by the devil or be content with complacency and mediocrity, thus not fulfilling the call of God on our lives. Not at all. We are to work to improve ourselves while at the same time remaining totally dependent on God.

Self-sufficiency means to be "sufficient in oneself," and not putting your faith in God's assistance. Contentment, on the other hand, is to know with certainty and absolute firm conviction that God is able to meet your every need; that He, Jehovah, is your all sufficiency.

YOU CAN FULFILL GOD'S PURPOSE WITH THE STRENGTH OF CHRIST!

Contentment means that you are aware that you don't covet another person's position, property, possessions, or personality. Why? Because you know and are assured that all you presently have and all that you are today is more than enough in the hands of God. Whatever you need to do to fulfill God's purpose you can do—not in your own strength—but through the strength and power of Christ that dwells within your innermost being.

The apostle Paul said:

*I know how to be abased, and I know how to abound. Everywhere and in all things I have learned both to be full and to be hungry, both to abound and to suffer need. **I can do all things through Christ who strengthens me*** (Philippians 4:12-13).

Where Confusion Reigns

In Nebuchadnezzar's case, the only help for him was repentance. Until he was able to look again to the Father for guidance and to recognize the Lord as his source, he was left in a world of insanity.

You may not enter into a world of insanity like Nebuchadnezzar, but the covering of God will be removed if you allow yourself to fall into an unprotected state. If you refuse to acknowledge that you have fallen and are separated from God, who is the eternal source of your supply, you will find yourself in a fallen condition, unable to get up.

> *But your iniquities have separated you from your God; and your sins have hidden His face from you, so that He will not hear* (Isaiah 59:2).

Like Nebuchadnezzar, you may refuse to ask for God's help. As a result, confusion will reign in your life. *"For God is **not** the author of confusion but of peace, as in all the churches of the saints"* (1 Cor. 14:33).

Nebuchadnezzar's pride and rebellion caused him to lose his kingship until he was willing to acknowledge God.

> *At the end of the time I, Nebuchadnezzar lifted my eyes to heaven, and my understanding returned to me; and I blessed the Most High and praised and honored Him who lives forever....At the same time my reason returned to me, ...I was restored to my kingdom, and excellent majesty was added to me. Now I...praise and extol and honor the King of heaven, all of whose works are truth, and His ways justice. And those who walk in pride He is able to put down* (Daniel 4:34,36-37).

Repentance was the key to Nebuchadnezzar's healing and deliverance. When he acknowledged his pride and began to praise and honor God, his mind was restored. But the great king never forgot that God is able to bring low those who "walk in pride."

To fall is bad enough, but to fall and not cry out for help, refusing to repent for your sin, is worse than the fall itself. Some people are so full of pride and consumed with their own self-sufficiency that they think, "If I can't get up myself, I won't let anyone help me."

Maybe you are ashamed to let anyone know that you have fallen, because you don't want them to think less of you. It is especially difficult to ask for help if you have led people to believe that you are some great, spiritual giant, incapable of falling from your high and lofty place.

STOP BEING SO PROUD.

Is your image so important that you're willing to continue in your pitiful fallen state? Are you so deceived that you will not acknowledge that you have sinned? Stop being so proud. After all, isn't that what caused you to fall in the first place?

Pride is dangerous because it forces you to lie needlessly in a helpless state for days—and sometimes years. If you had asked for help immediately, you could have gotten up and gone on with your life.

The Way Back

King David began his descent into sin when he lusted for a woman who was not his wife and committed adultery. When Bathsheba became pregnant with his child, David set up her husband to be killed.

The Lord sent Nathan, the prophet of God, to reveal and convict David of his sins:

Why have you despised the commandment of the LORD, to do evil in His sight? You have killed Uriah the Hittite with the sword; you have taken his wife to be your wife, and have killed him with the sword of the people of Ammon (2 Samuel 12:9).

David, realizing that God knows and sees all things, replied with great sorrow and remorse, "I have sinned against the Lord."

The Lord spared David's life, but the child that he and Bathsheba conceived died. When David repented of his sins, God picked David up and put him back on his feet.

What if King David had not acknowledged and confessed his sins even after the prophet came to him? What if David had been so full of pride and denial that he would have allowed his kingdom to be destroyed before ever asking God for forgiveness?

NEVER BE TOO PRIDEFUL TO ASK FOR FORGIVENESS.

Many are so bound by pride that you would rather let everything significant be destroyed and diminished by the devil rather than ask God for help. Some people are so prideful that they reject help even when the Lord prompts someone to give it.

We need to be more like David. When we realize we have fallen, we must repent immediately! We need to repent with urgency and sincerity as Kind David did.

Don't allow satan to deceive you into thinking that because no one saw you commit your sin, you don't have to repent. That deception will cause you to stay in a fallen state. *Don't allow pride to lock you into a state of unforgiveness.*

At times, we fall and are unable to get up or even ask for help. At other times, we have fallen and just do not want to get up and try again because we are afraid we might fall again. Do not stop trying. Like the woman in the medical alert commercial, when you've fallen, scream with urgency: "Lord, help! I've fallen, and I can't get up!"

Stamina Secrets and Solutions

1. "Pride has caused the fall of many great and gifted individuals." Do you know people who have fallen from a prestigious position because of pride? Have you ever had a prideful slip?

   _____

   _____

   _____

   _____

2. Have you been blinded to the truth by pride? Pride prevents the proud from viewing life realistically. What's your view of life?

   _____

   _____

   _____

   _____

3. To whom or what do you give credit for the success you are experiencing? Career? Family? Business? Ministry? Parents? Church leadership? God?

   _____

   _____

   _____

   _____

4. "Repentance was the key to Nebuchadnezzar's healing and deliverance." If you are feeling confused or your mind is baffled, seriously consider that you need to repent. You are assured of healing and deliverance from a faithful God Almighty.

_____

_____

_____

_____

5. When you realize you have fallen, you must repent immediately! Jesus will immediately reach out His arms and catch you. Of this you can be sure. Are you?

_____

_____

_____

_____

CHAPTER 4

In Your Darkest Hour

*There is a way that seems right to a man, but its
end is the way of death* (Proverbs 14:12).

Are you fighting against God? Maybe you have struggled in
your mind, wondering: *Should I ask for help? Who would be
willing to help me? What if they laugh at me?* You find yourself trying to get help from everyone—except God.

Giving Up the Fight

The apostle Paul, who was formerly named Saul of Tarsus,
had persecuted many Christians out of religious zeal. He, too,
found it hard to accept the fact that he needed help.

*And as he journeyed, he came near Damascus: and sud-
denly there shined round about him a light from heaven:
and he fell to the earth, and heard a voice saying unto him,
Saul, Saul, why persecutest thou Me? And he said, Who
art Thou, Lord? And the Lord said, I am Jesus whom thou*

persecutest: it is hard for thee to kick against the pricks (Acts 9:3-5 KJV).

What did Jesus mean when He said, *"I am Jesus whom thou persecutest: it is hard for thee to kick against the pricks"?*

The word "prick" is the King James translation for the word "goad." Goad means "to sting; a form of aggressive agitation." Today, we say, "He tried to goad me into a fight."

In this passage from Acts, "prick" is used metaphorically to represent the prompting and pricking of the Holy Spirit that God had allowed to come upon Saul's life in an effort to get his attention. The Lord was trying to show Saul that spiritually, he was going down the wrong road and moving in a direction contrary to God's will.

> *As he journeyed he came near Damascus, and suddenly a light shone around him from heaven. Then he fell to the ground, and heard a voice saying to him, "Saul, Saul, why are you persecuting Me?" And he said, "Who are You, Lord?" Then the Lord said, "I am Jesus, whom you are persecuting. It is hard for you to kick against the goads"* (Acts 9:3-5).

Stubborn and hard-headed, Saul insisted on doing things his own way. After all, he was intelligent, capable, religious—and proud of it! As a result, it took a dramatic move of God to knock Saul off his "high horse."

After being blinded by the bright light, this radical zealot found himself in the humble position of needing someone to lead him by the hand. This temporary loss of sight was God's way of showing Saul there was Someone far greater than he.

> *Then Saul arose from the ground, and when his eyes were opened he saw no one. But they led him by the hand and brought him into Damascus. And he was three days without sight, and neither ate nor drank* (Acts 9:8-9).

God was saying, "Saul, why do you kick against the pricks?" In other words, "Why do you fight against what you know is true? Why do you insist on doing things your own way without first consulting Me?"

Is the Lord asking you the same question, "Why do you kick against the pricks?" The American translation puts it this way, *"Why do you allow yourself to continue to run into brick walls?"*

These brick walls represent sin and rebellion. Why do we continue to allow satan to deceive us into following him? No matter how sane and rational the sin may seem to you, sin is sin.

Sin always separates us from the presence of God. What a price to pay for wanting things our own way!

In Your Time of Need

Like Saul, we sometimes find ourselves in need of not only divine but human assistance. In fact, God usually sends other people to help us in our time of need.

Blinded for three days, Saul was so depressed he couldn't eat or drink anything. At the same time that Saul thought he had reached his darkest hour, God was preparing a man named Ananias to minister to Saul.

> *And there was a certain disciple at Damascus, named Ananias; and to him said the Lord in a vision, Ananias. And he said, Behold, I am here, Lord. And the Lord said unto him, Arise, and go into the street which is called Straight, and inquire in the house of Judas for one called Saul, of Tarsus: for, behold, he prayeth, and hath seen in a vision a man named Ananias coming in, and putting his hand on him, that he might receive his sight. …And Ananias went his way, and entered into the house; and putting his hands on him said, Brother Saul,* **the Lord,** *even Jesus, that appeared unto thee in the way as thou camest,* **hast sent me, that thou mightest receive thy sight, and be filled with the Holy Ghost.** *And*

immediately there fell from his eyes as it had been scales:
and he received sight forthwith, and arose, and was baptized
(Acts 9:10-12,17-18 KJV).

If you are in a place where you need God's divine assistance, ask the Lord to send someone to help you. There may already be people in your life who are available to bring healing and deliverance to you.

You must, however, be willing to submit, as Saul did, to their ministry. Don't fight divine connections! There is nothing to fear; God will not allow you to be hurt again.

Have you ever noticed the way zoo caretakers handle an injured animal? Even though the caretaker is only interested in helping, the animal does not understand. It only focuses on the pain and, because of this, it will strike or even kill the very person sent to help it.

Some of you may be in this very state. People who have called themselves Christians have done hurtful things to you. You did not expect them to be the ones inflicting the pain. It seemed to hurt far worse because these people professed to love the Lord.

GOD WANTS TO DELIVER YOU!

You may have been hurt to such an extent that you no longer trust anybody, not even God. You may not have actually said, "Lord, I don't trust You," but your actions speak louder than words. Maybe you avoid reading God's Word or refuse to allow anyone to pray for you. Do you look for other ways to help alleviate and drown the pain?

Therefore if the Son makes you free, you shall be free indeed
(John 8:36).

God wants to deliver you! He wants to arrest every stronghold and every demonic spirit in your life—every demonic power, every type of sorcery, every hex, every spirit of unbelief, every spirit of doubt, every spirit of pride. God wants you set free, now!

Profile of the Fallen

What causes someone to fall? Have you experienced something so traumatic and life-changing that you have fallen away from God and forsaken the love of the Father?

Are you one of those saints who was once consumed with doing His will and only His will? Do you now haphazardly serve Him? Were you once preoccupied with spending long hours in conversation with the Lord, but you are now without time to even read His Word? Were you once consumed with the very essence of praise and worship to the Father but now opt to live without praise, except for those times of great need?

> *I have fought the good fight, I have finished the race, I have kept the faith* (2 Timothy 4:7).

Many people fall because they are no longer grafted into the Father. They do not seek His wisdom. Without God's wisdom and the fullness of His Spirit, saints become self-deceived, self-promoting, and just plain carnal and fleshly, thinking only of self. They fool themselves into thinking they can recover by themselves without God's divine intervention or His ordained supernatural human assistance.

Maybe you've given up the fight. Deep in your inner man you have fainted in your spiritual life. You have complained about things you wanted to do but couldn't perform.

God has never said anything that He could not perform. Whether it was, "Let there be light" or "Lazarus come forth," if God said it, He always backed it up by His power and His Spirit.

Before God commissioned Moses to deliver the children of Israel out of Egyptian bondage, He first told him, *"I Am that I Am."*

If you're going to continually live a life of victory, the first thing you have got to know is that "God is able."

> *...he who comes to God must believe that He is, and that He is a rewarder of those who diligently seek Him* (Hebrews 11:6).

God says, "Do you not know or at least have you not heard, that I am God, the Maker of Heaven and earth and I change not?" In other words, God says, "There is no fainting with Me; there's no failure in Me. I AM THAT I AM."

> *...God resists the proud, but gives grace to the humble* (James 4:6).

When you get through searching and trying other things, you're still going to have to come back to God because He holds the power, and He has your answer. It is up to you to humble yourself and say, "Lord, help! I've fallen, and I can't get up!"

Struggling in Vain

Have you been living with one foot in and one foot out of God's Kingdom, giving God a "maybe," instead of "yes"? If so, it is time to stop struggling. The Holy Ghost is after you; He is in hot pursuit.

The Bible says, *"At the name of Jesus every knee should bow... and that every tongue should confess that Jesus Christ is Lord, to the glory of God the Father"* (Phil. 2:10-11). So why wait to be brought to your knees? Acknowledge Jesus as Lord of your life today. It will save you a lot of pain and sorrow.

> *Have ye not known? have ye not heard? hath it not been told you from the beginning? have ye not understood from*

the foundations of the earth? It is He that sitteth upon the circle of the earth, and the inhabitants thereof are as grasshoppers; that stretcheth out the heavens as a curtain, and spreadeth them out as a tent to dwell in: that bringeth the princes to nothing; He maketh the judges of the earth as vanity. ...To whom then will ye liken Me, or shall I be equal? saith the Holy One. Lift up your eyes on high, and behold who hath created these things, that bringeth out their host by number: He calleth them all by names by the greatness of His might, for that He is strong in power; not one faileth. Why sayest thou, O Jacob, and speakest, O Israel, My way is hid from the LORD, and my judgment is passed over from my God? Hast thou not known? hast thou not heard, that the everlasting God, the LORD, the Creator of the ends of the earth, fainteth not, neither is weary? there is no searching of His understanding. He giveth power to the faint; and to them that have no might He increaseth strength. Even the youths shall faint and be weary, and the young men shall utterly fall: **but they that wait upon the LORD shall renew their strength; they shall mount up with wings as eagles; they shall run, and not be weary; and they shall walk, and not faint** (Isaiah 40:21-23,25-31 KJV).

When your pity party is over and you are ready for His help, God will say, "Don't you know? Have you not heard who I am— the everlasting God? I am the Creator of the universe. I am not a child; I am not a school boy—I am God. Who do you think you're fooling? I'm God. I hold your breath in My hands. I created your body. I heat your blood just hot enough to keep you alive, but not so hot that you die. I'm God. I measured your life in the sands of My own hand. I'm God. Why would you serve anybody else? Who else do you allow to control your life? If it is not Me, then who? I love you. I created you in My image. I am that I am."

DON'T LET SATAN FOOL YOU.

Why do you continue in this fallen state? What more does the Lord have to do or say to show you He loves you? Don't let satan continue to fool you into thinking that God has forsaken you.

Stop blaming others for your mistakes. Realize and admit that there is something wrong with you. Quit being mad at everyone and stop trying to adjust the whole world to fit your circumstances.

Jesus answered, "Most assuredly, I say to you, unless one is born of water and the Spirit, he cannot enter the kingdom of God" (John 3:5).

When some folks go down, they want to lower the standard for everyone else. They want everything to fit into their world. They want to start calling wrong, right, and calling right, wrong.

Stop doing things that you know you don't have any business doing. Repent and confess your sins instead of spending your time pointing out the sins of everyone else. Admit that you have fallen so that your healing may begin.

When Jesus heard it, He said to them, "Those who are well have no need of a physician, but those who are sick. I did not come to call the righteous, but sinners, to repentance" (Mark 2:17).

Repent therefore and be converted, that your sins may be blotted out, so that times of refreshing may come from the presence of the Lord (Acts 3:19).

Stop running into those brick walls. Die to your pride and ask for help! He will help you and restore you to your former state. Just ask for help. Let your heart be opened to God. He will be there for you, even in your darkest hour.

Stamina Secrets and Solutions

1. "Are you fighting against God?" You may not realize it, but are you resisting God's will in your life? What steps can you take to ensure you are walking in your God-given destiny?

_____

_____

_____

_____

2. Sin always separates you from the presence of God. What price are you willing to pay for wanting things your own way?

_____

_____

_____

_____

3. Have you fainted in your spiritual life? How often do you read God's Word for encouragement and motivation? How recently have you knelt before Him in humbleness and asked for His forgiveness?

_____

_____

_____

_____

4. Do you believe that the Holy Spirit is in hot pursuit of you? Are you running toward Him or away from Him? Why?

_____

_____

_____

5. Are you mad at everyone and trying to adjust the world to fit your circumstances? When you really believe that God loves you and will work out everything to your benefit, your anger will disappear. Believe now.

_____

_____

_____

CHAPTER 5

Asking *Why?*

I was taught not to ask God, "Why?" I was taught that true Christians never ask God *why?* It was considered a breech of our faith to ask God *why?* If you really believe God, you just completely accept everything that comes your way without asking God anything pertaining to its reason for happening: It's as if God gets insulted, mad, or feels like you're questioning His authority when you ask Him *why?*

Others feel that if you ask why, God is intimidated with your quest for knowledge or that you might ask Him something that He cannot answer or that you might offend or hinder God's ability to be omniscient. For whatever the reason, you just don't ask Almighty God, *why?*

However, the Bible says, *"If any of you lacks wisdom, let him ask of God, who gives to all liberally and without reproach"* (James 1:5). God said, "Come to Me and ask Me why." He said, "I'm not afraid of your questions. I'm not afraid of you." God is not insecure in His sovereignty. He's not envious of man or afraid that His position, power, or authority is going to be jeopardized by you or anybody else knowing too much.

IF YOU LACK WISDOM, ASK GOD!

I don't care how many times you have to ask Him. He says ask of Him who gives freely as He wills. God said, "When you are confused, your mind is perplexed, your heart is troubled, and you don't know what-in-the-world to do, come to Me and ask Me. Lay all the cards down on the table. Say, this is happening and that is happening. There's trouble here and there's trouble there. There's trouble everywhere. I've been serving You all I know how, and it looks like things are getting worse instead of better. God, why?"

God says He can handle it. Bring it to Him. "I'm able," says God, "to share with you the kind of truth that transforms." God says, "Cry out to Me; inquire of Me. Knock and the door shall be opened, seek and ye shall find."

Faith in God, the Key to Answered Prayers

God says when you've searched for Him with your whole heart (your entire being), then you will find Him. If we are serious about hearing from God, we're going to have to exercise the kind of faith that is strong and persistent just like the woman in Jesus' parable about the unjust judge.

Then He spoke a parable to them, that men always ought to pray and not lose heart, saying: "There was in a certain city a judge who did not fear God nor regard man. Now there was a widow in that city; and she came to him, saying, 'Get justice for me from my adversary.' And he would not for a while; but afterward he said within himself, 'Though I do not fear God nor regard man, yet because this widow troubles me I will avenge her, lest by her continual coming she weary me.'"

Then the Lord said, "Hear what the unjust judge said. And shall God not avenge His own elect who cry out day and night to Him, though He bears long with them? I tell you that He will avenge them speedily. Nevertheless, when the Son of Man comes, will He really find faith on the earth?" (Luke 18:1-8).

The judge did not want to hear the woman's plea for justice, but the woman pressed him so hard and so long that he granted the woman's request. The judge did this not because he felt sorry for her or had compassion on her, but the judge granted her petition simply because the lady literally "got on his nerves."

The widow, realizing the judge's reluctance and refusal to hear her, could have lost hope, lost faith, and simply given up. But the woman was persistent, and her persistence was actually fueled and empowered by her faith; a faith that declares, "I don't care how long it takes; I don't care what I have to suffer or what pain I must endure; I don't care who doesn't agree with me or doesn't like me for believing God; I know that if I keep on keeping on, one day, sooner or later, my change is going to come and I will see the salvation of the Lord."

Regardless of the excesses and some erroneous teachings that have been associated with the "Word of Faith" and Charismatic movements, Christians must forever remember and be mindful of the fact that the Word of God declares that anything in our life that is not rooted in or brought about by faith in the Almighty, is sin. For, without faith it is impossible to please God. The just (righteous men and women of God) shall and must live by faith.

*For in it the righteousness of God is revealed from faith to faith; as it is written, "**The just shall live by faith**"* (Romans 1:17).

I have been crucified with Christ; it is no longer I who live, but Christ lives in me; and the life which I now live in the *flesh I **live by faith** in the Son of God, who loved me and gave Himself for me* (Galatians 2:20).

*Now the just shall **live by faith**; but if anyone draws back, My soul has no pleasure in him* (Hebrews 10:38).

Faith for the believer is what gasoline is for an automobile; it's what electricity is for lights and high-powered appliances. It (faith in God and confidence in self) is what fuels our lives and gives motivation, inspiration, and eternal hope for our existence.

WITHOUT FAITH IT IS IMPOSSIBLE TO PLEASE GOD.

As the motivational and inspirational speaker Les Brown says about faith in God and in self:

Within you lies the power to seize the hour and live your dreams. Faith is the oil that takes the friction out of living. Faith will enable you to turn liabilities into assets and stumbling blocks into stepping stones. When you begin to have faith, your load will get heavy but your knees won't buckle, you'll get knocked down but you won't get knocked out. You've got to have faith if you are going to make it in life. You must believe in yourself and in a power greater than yourself, and do your best and don't worry about the rest. You must maintain faith and work as if everything depended on you, and pray as if everything depended on God.

Please, let me be clear on what faith is, so that you make no mistakes about what I'm talking about. I'm not talking about some kind of feel-good confession rooted in humanism, saying, "I'm OK, you're OK." Nor am I referring to some kind of manipulation of Scripture to formulate my recipe for success. That's a form of Charismatic witchcraft, and I don't associate with witches. No! When I say, "faith," I'm talking about complete, absolute, uncompromising trust in God. It is a faith that knows my successes in life are not because of some great wonderful ability of my own, but my help comes from the Lord.

> *I will lift up my eyes to the hills—from whence comes my help? My help comes from the* LORD, *Who made heaven and earth* (Psalm 121:1-2).

For He, the Lord God Almighty, enables me to do His good will and all things for His good pleasure. It is God who works all things and does all things together for our good. In accordance with His calling on our lives and His overall purpose for humankind, He does these things (trials as well as blessings) as prerequisites of our love for Him. Love directed toward God is reflected and expressed by our obedience to His Word and submission to His commands:

> *By this we know that we love the children of God, when we love God and keep His commandments. For this is the love of God, that we keep His commandments. And His commandments are not burdensome* (1 John 5:2-3).

We must know that the supreme principle of faith is the product of God's love toward us, *"faith working through love"* (Gal. 5:6).

GOD WORKS ALL THINGS TOGETHER FOR YOUR GOOD.

We often trust only people we know love us, people in whom we are assured have our best interest at heart. With agape love, the recipient's welfare is always the giver's number one concern. Knowing this makes it easier to trust the heavenly Father, the One who loved you while you were yet a sinner, unworthy of love. Having promised that He will never leave or forsake us, no matter how difficult the circumstances, or how severe the situation, we are not without hope. Our hope makes us not ashamed *"because the love of God is shed abroad in our hearts by the Holy Ghost which is given unto us"* (Rom. 5:5 KJV). Faith works by love.

Patience and Waiting on God

The problem with most Christians is that we are far too impatient. If God doesn't speak in the first five minutes of our prayer time, we get up, shake ourselves off, and concede that God is not talking today. We no longer have the kind of tenacity, diligence, and persistence like the saints of old. Those saints of bygone days would get on their faces before God and grab hold of the horns of the altar and refuse to let go until they received a sure word from God.

Unlike those precious men and women of God, we have become the "microwave" generation. We want everything overnight, even Christian maturity. We want whatever is quick, fast, and in a hurry. We've deleted, erased, and totally obliterated from our Bibles, and our thoughts, those passages of Scripture that command us to wait on God during turbulent, troubling, and unsure times.

> *My brethren, count it all joy when you fall into various trials, knowing that the testing of your faith produces patience. But let patience have its perfect work, that you may be perfect and complete, lacking nothing* (James 1:2-4).

You might ask me, "Bishop, why (there's that why again) does it often take God so long to answer my prayers?" We put a petition, request, or question before God on a Monday, and it might be the next week or next month before God gives a reply. This tests our faith in order to see if we will continue to serve God, even if He delays His reply. If God decides to prolong an answer or provision for our needs, are we willing and secure enough in His sovereignty to trust and wait on Him, regardless of how bleak the situation may look? My brothers and sisters, we have to let patience have its perfect (complete, absolute, to full maturity) work.

God's reply to the nagging questions and complex issues that preoccupy our thoughts is, "I may not answer you right away, but go ahead and question why, and wait on Me."

> *But those who wait on the LORD shall renew their strength; they shall mount up with wings like eagles; they shall run and not be weary, they shall walk and not faint* (Isaiah 40:31).

What are you waiting for? I'm waiting for an answer. Does your vision tarry? Wait for it. Be diligent. Don't become weary in well doing; for in due season you shall reap the reward of your request, your petition, your labor, and the answers to your whys if you faint not:

> *And let us not grow weary while doing good, for in due season we shall reap if we do not lose heart* (Galatians 6:9).

Has God told you that He has destined you for a certain thing? Has God given you a vision of ministry? Has He promised you a particular blessing? Maybe you're single and God has assured you that you'll be married at an appointed time. But it seems as if the mate that God has fitted for your specific needs is nowhere in sight.

If any of these predicaments are your present experience, I remind you of what God told His prophet Habakkuk. At a time when the prophet was despondent because of what he had seen and experienced, God said:

Write the vision and make it plain on tablets, that he [you] may run who reads it. For the vision is yet for an appointed time; but at the end it will speak, and it will not lie. Though it tarries, wait for it; because it will surely come, it will not tarry (Habakkuk 2:2-3).

If God has spoken to you about your life and has shown you a glorious end to the matter, wait on it. If, in your waiting, you exercise faith, prayer, and patience, the vision shall surely come to pass. The Lord your God is not a man that He should lie nor the son of man that He should repent. God says:

I know the thoughts that I think toward you...thoughts of peace, and not of evil, to give you an expected end. Then shall ye call upon me, and ye shall go and pray unto me, and I will hearken unto you. And ye shall seek me, and find me, when ye shall search for me with all your heart. And I will be found of you...and I will turn away your captivity (Jeremiah 29:11-14a KJV).

Tribulations Work Patience

Therefore being justified by faith, we have peace with God through our Lord Jesus Christ: by whom also we have access by faith into this grace wherein we stand, and rejoice in hope of the glory of God. And not only so, but we glory in tribulations also: knowing that tribulation worketh patience (Romans 5:1-3 KJV).

Patience, contrary to popular belief, is not the same as waiting. Waiting is a passive posture but patience is an active principle. Waiting, by itself, is by no means a guarantee of receiving the promise God has for your life. If that were the case, the five virgins in the Bible, caught without oil in their lamps, would have been ready at the Lord's coming.

PATIENCE IS NOT THE SAME AS WAITING.

Also, the Hebrews who came out of Egypt would have entered the Promised Land. No! Patience is not just "waiting on God." Patience is based on the scriptural principle of persistence and perseverance (steadfastness in delay). Patience also does not come by prayer alone. As a matter of fact, a prayer for patience is only an acknowledgment of your lack of it and does not mean God will grant your request through a supernatural gift. No! My brother and sister, I wish it was that easy. As a matter of fact, when you ask God for patience, you only get it as a by-product of something else that the Lord sends your way. Are you curious to know what that something else is? (I know you are!) It is tribulation.

Tribulation. There is absolutely no other God-given way to grow in the fruit of patience. Trib-u-la-tion. The word even sounds funny and undesirable, but it's a necessary element of Christian perfection and a primary prerequisite in receiving the promises of God.

Tribulation. What is it? What does it mean? Is it affliction? Does it mean I'm going to have to suffer? Yes!

Tribulation means all of these and many other undesirable and unwelcome things that I will discuss in a later chapter. But without exercising patience we will not be able to receive the full counsel of the Lord, nor will we see the vision of God in our lives come to pass. There will be no patience without tribulation.

THERE IS NO PATIENCE
WITHOUT TRIBULATION.

Many times we pray for things, but we don't recognize or understand the answer to our prayers. Remember, in all things God has a divine process and order by which He operates everything on the earth.

We ask for strength, and God sends us difficult situations to make us strong. We pray for wisdom, and God provides us with problems that provoke us to come up with solutions and develop wisdom. We ask for prosperity, and God gives us strength to work and wisdom to invent. We ask for a favor, and God gives us responsibility. A large percentage of our success is the result of our eating the bread of adversity and drinking the bitter waters of affliction.

The genius of success is to be able to see the good that hides in every situation. As a pessimist sees obstacles in his opportunities, so an optimist sees opportunities in his obstacles. Tribulation works patience.

Stamina Secrets and Solutions

1. As a child or a new Christian, were you told not to ask God *why?* Do you believe that God gets insulted, mad, or feels like you're questioning His authority when you ask Him *why?*

   _____

   _____

   _____

   _____

2. "There's trouble here and there's trouble there. There's trouble everywhere. I've been serving You all I know how, and it looks like things are getting worse instead of better. God, why?" Have you been in this situation? God wants you to keep asking Him for the answer—He will give it to you.

   _____

   _____

   _____

   _____

3. He will never leave or forsake you, no matter how difficult the circumstances, or how severe the situation, you are not without hope. Memorize this truth.

   _____

   _____

   _____

4. "Waiting is a passive posture but patience is an active principle." Are you better at waiting or being patient? Why?

_____

_____

_____

5. Without exercising patience you will not receive the full counsel of the Lord, nor will you see the vision of God in your life come to pass. Determine to be more patient today and every day.

_____

_____

_____

CHAPTER 6

God's School of the Spirit

Any teacher will tell you that education begins not with lectures or speeches, but with interaction with the pupil. The classes are not really good until the teacher has sufficiently stimulated the students to the point where they begin to ask questions about the subject being studied. With hands raised, they ask the teacher, *why?* Then the explanation process begins. Before you know it, you have a serious dialogue going on, all centered on the inquisition, *why?*

As the teacher explains, she establishes a relationship with the student. The teacher knows she has the student in the palms of her hands. If she can get you to ask a question, she has motivated you. When you ask why, you're saying, "I'm interested in what you're doing." At that precise moment, the teacher has engaged you (the student) not only in the education process, but in the actual learning experience.

Teachers who successfully continue in the educating process not only must establish a dialogue with the student, but also must adequately and competently answer complex, difficult, and perplexing questions in the minds of students. The student's line of questioning, from that point, begins to convey a message that says, "I respect your ability as a teacher to be able to give me answers." At this stage in the educational process, trust begins. If the teacher has proven continually that he or she has the student's personal, as well as academic, interest in mind, the learning process advances to the pivotal and the most warranted stage referred to as discipleship.

> *Now it happened, as Jesus sat at the table in the house, that behold, many tax collectors and sinners came and sat down with Him and His disciples. And when the Pharisees saw it, they said to His disciples, "Why does your **Teacher** eat with tax collectors and sinners?" When Jesus heard that, He said to them, "Those who are well have no need of a physician, but those who are sick. **But go and learn what this means:** 'I desire mercy and not sacrifice.' For I did not come to call the righteous, but sinners, to repentance"* (Matthew 9:10-13).

From that point on, the student communicates to the teacher that through their relationship he wants an exchange. Not only an exchange of answers, but for the teacher to teach him how to reason like a teacher. Therefore, this exchange will enable the student to become a teacher and ultimately teach other people. This is what God really desires and wishes to share with us as disciples of Christ.

THE STUDENT BECOMES THE TEACHER.

God desires all His children to have intimate dialogues with Him, like He had with Adam and Eve before the fall of man. God, our heavenly Father, still seeks to walk with us in the cool of the day. Contrary to erroneous beliefs, God has always sought to communicate with His most blessed and highest earthly creation— humankind. God wants to communicate with us, which is one of the primary reasons He sent the Holy Spirit to commune with us so that we might learn something of His ways and purposes. The Scripture declares that:

> *...you do not need that anyone teach you; but as the same anointing teaches you concerning all things, and is true, and is not a lie, and just as it has taught you, you will abide in Him* (1 John 2:27).

Just as college professors relate to students, God, by His Spirit, wants to have the same exchange with us. God's desire is to be with us, to work with us, to shape and mold us, to convene and plan with us, and to deal with us until we get to the point that we grow up from being students and become teachers ourselves.

> *That we henceforth be no more children, tossed to and fro, and carried about with every wind of doctrine, by the sleight* [trickery] *of men, and cunning craftiness, whereby they lie in wait to deceive; but speaking the truth in love, may grow up into Him in all things, which is the head, even Christ* (Ephesians 4:14-15 KJV).

Teachers are able to impart wisdom to potential students and wisdom one to another, thus the *School of the Spirit*.

Teacher's Pet

There's no way that you can be the kind of student who goes into overtime and not become the teacher's pet. Remember seeing them in school? They were those students who always were in the teacher's face, and the teacher just loved them. They always asked why, as if everything the teacher discussed was so interesting. You were probably like me, always so bored and so sick of them, you wanted to hit them in the head with an apple. They just kept asking, *why?* and the teacher seemed to enjoy them so much.

They had established that teacher-to-student, student-to-teacher relationship.

God says, "Don't sit in My class and be reluctant to ask questions. I'm the Master Teacher, the Good Master Teacher." God says, "If you really want to know, ask Me, and I will give you the heathen for an inheritance..." (see Ps. 2:8). "If you really want to get something going with Me, start draining from the milk of My wisdom, start pulling from Me. Ask and it shall be given; knock, and the door shall be open unto you; seek, and ye shall find" (see Matt. 7:7).

"IF YOU REALLY WANT TO KNOW ME, ASK ME."

God wants us to be inquisitive. He's tired of His children being passive and just accepting everything that comes into our lives. He wants us to question Him that we may find clarity and find effective solutions to the problems confronting us day in and day out. He wants you to take a stand and start asking *why?* He's tired of us lying down and saying, "This is the way it's got to be. I don't think there's any way it's going to change." God said, "I want you to contest Me, and ask *why?*"

Peter, the Master Teacher's Pet

The earthly ministry of Jesus began with Him teaching, training, developing, and mentoring 12 men. The Bible refers to them as disciples. The word "disciple" comes from the Greek word *mathetes*, which means a learner or student.

It was the tradition of Jesus' day that disciples not only learned from the teacher's lectures and discourses, but also by observing and experiencing every aspect of the teacher's very life. The disciples literally lived with the teacher. They actually watched everything the teacher did. The disciples listened to everything the teacher said. They ate with Him and traveled with Him. The disciples were in close proximity with each and every personal aspect of Jesus' (the Master Teacher's) life.

The Church exists today as a result of the obedience and faithfulness of those 12 men, minus one (Judas). So it is quite evident that Jesus was an enormously good, proficient, and effective Teacher for 11 of His 12 men to go on and change the entire world and course of all humankind. No other teacher, school, or university can claim such success and effectiveness.

However, out of the 12 men, one stood out above all the rest. Peter. He later became known as the apostle Peter, the one Jesus called a rock. A very unique and passionate quality about this disciple distinguished him from the other 11. That quality was Peter's dogged determination to understand issues. He was known for always asking, *why?*

No doubt, the other disciples thought Peter was a big mouth. They probably said he talked too much. They probably felt that Peter thought he was a know-it-all, but it was Peter's tendency to always ask why that caused Jesus, the Teacher, to notice this loud-mouthed man and reward him with the much desired position of Teacher's pet. Notice, I said reward and not appoint.

ARE YOU THE TEACHER'S PET?

You may be appointed to be a disciple but you have to earn the right—through diligence to know truth—to be the Teacher's pet. That's why Jesus chose Peter. Jesus knew that if enough of Peter's whys were answered, then the loudmouthed, nosey, obnoxious fisherman would eventually become a great leader and apostle that God could use to get the world's attention.

God is no respecter of persons. He does not grant favor or special privileges based on human ability or earthly accomplishments. God does show favor to those who hunger and thirst for righteousness. God favors those who thirst to know the truth and desire, no matter how great the cost, to do the will of God. It is evident that Jesus gave more attention to the development of three of the disciples—Peter, James, and John. But there was something extra significant about the relationship between Jesus and Peter, and that's what was so significant, the fact that they had a relationship.

> *Jesus answered and said to him, "Blessed are you, Simon Bar-Jonah* [Peter], *for flesh and blood has not revealed this to you, but My Father who is in heaven. And I also say to you that **you are Peter, and on this rock I will build My church,** and the gates of Hades shall not prevail against it. And I will give you the keys of the kingdom of heaven, and whatever you bind on earth will be bound in heaven, and whatever you loose on earth will be loosed in heaven"* (Matthew 16:17-19).

Through Peter's persistence in asking questions, he initiated an exchange that developed a relationship between student and teacher. It caused the Teacher to spend special time with the student. Every time something sacred and significant happened in Jesus' life and ministry, Peter was there. When Moses and Elijah appeared on the Mount of Transfiguration, who was there? When Jesus raised the little girl from the dead, He put everybody, including the family, out of the room, except for three of His disciples. Who was one of those disciples? Yes, you guessed it, Peter! Everywhere and every time something exciting was going on in Jesus' life and ministry, Simon Peter was there.

GOD LOVES ALL HIS CHILDREN.

Why would God spend special time with one student or child of God in comparison to any other child of God? Isn't that showing partiality? Does not God love all His children just the same? The answer to that question is yes, God does love all His children with the same degree of love. But God is a wise businessman as well as the sovereign Lord. He spends extra time, not based upon His loving one more than any other, but because the Father God knows, as well as Jesus, that you invest more time in individuals who exhibit a greater desire to know the truth, operate in those truths, and wish to influence and persuade others with that truth.

GOD WILL ANSWER THE WHYS OF YOUR HEART.

God desires us to know His will more than we even want to know it. If we are willing to ask God why and let Him transform us into receiving His will, God will show us His favor and answer the whys of our heart.

Stamina Secrets and Solutions

1. "God desires all His children to have intimate dialogues with Him." Are you intimately communicating daily with God?

   _____

   _____

   _____

2. God sent the Holy Spirit to commune with you so that you might learn something of His ways and purposes. Have you been a willing student?

   _____

   _____

   _____

3. God wants you to question Him to find clarity and effective solutions to the problems confronting you day in and day out. If you are not in the habit of questioning God, do so beginning today.

   _____

   _____

4. God favors those who thirst to know the truth and desire, no matter how great the cost, to do the will of God. Are you thirsty?

   _____

   _____

5. God will invest more time in you if you exhibit a desire to know the truth, operate in those truths, and wish to influence and persuade others with that truth.

_____

_____

CHAPTER 7

The Cold Kiss of a Calloused Heart

Friendship is the last remaining sign of our fleeting childhood dreams. It is the final symptom of our youth that lingers around the shadows of our adult mind. It reminds us of the sweet taste of a chosen love. Different from family love, which is not chosen but accepted, this love develops like moss on the slippery edges of a creek. It emerges without warning. There is no date to remember. It just gradually grows until one day an acquaintance has graduated into a friend. Love is the graduation diploma, whether discussed or hinted.

It is real and powerful, sweet and bitter. It is fanciful, idealistic, and iridescent enough to shine in the chilly night of an aloof world that has somehow lost the ability to interpret or appreciate the value of a friend. Only occasionally in the course of a lifetime do we meet the kind of friend that is more than an acquaintance. This kind of kindred spirit feels as warm and fitting as an old house shoe, with its personalized contours impressed upon soft fabric for the benefit of weary feet.

The Search for True Friendship

The tragedy is that we all yearn for, but seldom acquire, true trust and covenant. The truth is that real relationship is hard work. Let no one deceive you; contouring the heart to beat with another requires extensive whittling to trim away the self-centeredness with which many of us have enveloped ourselves. It is like riding the bus. If you are going to have company riding with you, you must be willing to scoot over and rearrange to accommodate another person and the many parcels that he brings. Your actions in doing this express the importance of the other person.

Every relationship undergoes adjustments. The reason one relationship becomes more valuable than others is found in its ability to survive circumstances and endure realignments. We never know the magnitude of a relationship's strength until it is tested by some threatening force. There must be a strong adhesive that can withstand the pressure and not be weakened by outside forces.

Friends Despite Imperfections

Isn't that part of what we want from relationships? To know that you won't leave, regardless of what is encountered—even if you discover my worst imperfection and I disclose my deepest scars! Isn't the real question, "Can I be transparent with you, and be assured that my nudity has not altered your commitment to be my friend?" I know that someone reading this chapter has given up on friendship, with its many expenses and desertions. If you will not believe me, then believe the Word of God. It is possible to attain real abiding friendship.

A man of many companions may come to ruin, but there is a friend who sticks closer than a brother (Proverbs 18:24 NIV).

Incidentally, notice that this proverb clearly warns against many companions. It is dangerous to be polygamous—even with friendship. Having too many companions creates jealousy, absorbs time, and cheapens commitment. How many friends can you handle? The object is quality and not quantity. As we share with one another, we must be prepared to love each other's imperfections, even when those imperfections challenge our commitment. We must decide, at some point, whether or not we can love like God. God sees every imperfection we have (He cannot be deceived), yet He maintains His commitment to love the unlovely. Isn't that why we love Him so much? We are completely vulnerable to Him. He knows us, yet He understands and loves us!

HE KNOWS US, YET HE
UNDERSTANDS AND LOVES US!

Even natural blood ties don't always wear as well as heart ties. The Bible says there is a kind of friend that *"sticks closer than a brother"* (Prov. 18:24b). What a tremendous statement. This is why we must not allow our friendships to be easily uprooted—not only in our individual lives, but also collectively as the Body of Christ. Too often we have thrown away good people who did a bad thing. The tragedy is in the fact that we usually forget all the good a friend has done and dwell only on the one bad thing he did to damage us. Have you ever done something like that? The deeper question is this: Are you throwing away the whole car over a bad battery? Is there any possibility of repair? No way, huh? Then how does God ever love you? If He ever forgave you of your debts as you forgave your debtors, could you stand?

The obvious friend is the one who stands by you, honoring and affirming you. The obvious friend affirms your marriage and family. You cannot be a friend and not uphold the institution of marriage and family. A true friend should desire to see me prosper in my marriage, in my finances, and in my health and spirituality. If these virtues are present in the relationship, then we can easily climb over the hurdles of personal imperfection and, generally, are mature enough to support what supports us. We, in turn, transmit through fleeting smiles, handshakes, hugs and warm exchanges of mutual affection, our celebration of friendship and appreciation.

Acceptance Without Measure

What we all need is the unique gift of acceptance. Most of us fear the bitter taste of rejection, but perhaps worse than rejection is the naked pain that attacks an exposed heart when a relationship is challenged by some struggle.

THE OBVIOUS FRIEND IS THE ONE WHO STANDS BY YOU, HONORING AND AFFIRMING YOU.

Suppose I share my heart, my innermost thoughts, with someone who betrays me, and I am wounded again? The distress of betrayal can become a wall that insulates us, but it also isolates us from those around us. Yes, I must admit that there are good reasons for being protective and careful. I also admit that love is always a risk. Yet I still suggest that the risk is worth the reward! What a privilege to have savored the contemplations of idle moments with the tender eyes of someone whose glistening expression invites you like the glowing embers of a crackling fire.

Communication becomes needless between people who need no audible speech. Their speech is the quick glance and the soft pat on a shoulder. Their communication is a concerned glance when all is not well with you. If you have ever sunken down into the rich lather of a real covenant relationship, then you are wealthy.

This relationship is the wealth that causes street people to smile in the rain and laugh in the snow. They have no coats to warm them; their only flame is the friendship of someone who relates to the plight of daily living. In this regard, many wealthy people are impoverished. They have things, but they lack camaraderie. The greatest blessings are often void of expense, yet they provide memories that enrich the credibility of life's dreary existence.

You say, "I am rich; I have acquired wealth and do not need a thing." But you do not realize that you are wretched, pitiful, poor, blind and naked (Revelation 3:17 NIV).

Children understand the rich art of relationship. They are often angry, but their anger quickly dissipates in the glaring sunshine of a fresh opportunity to laugh and jest a day away. The hearts of most adults, however, have been blackened by unforgiveness. They will hold a club of remembered infractions against one another for long periods of time, perhaps for a lifetime. There is a vacancy in the hearts of most men that causes them to be narrow and superficial. This vacancy is the vast gap between casual relationships and intimate attachments. It is the gift of friendship that should fill the gap between these wide designated points of human relationship.

A Common Bond

Since there is no blood to form the basis of relativity between friends, the bond must exist through some other mode of reality. A commonality is needed to anchor the relationship of two individuals against the chilly winds of passing observers, whose suspicious minds activate and attempt to terminate any of your relationships. They are not accustomed to relationships outside of the junglelike, carnivorous stalkings of one another as prey. However, this bond may exist in an area that outsiders would never understand, but thank God their confusion doesn't dilute the intensity of admiration that exists between true friends.

Many people are surrounded by crowds of business people, coworkers, and even family members—yet they are alone. Disenchanted with life, they become professional actors on the stage of life. They do not allow anyone to get close, fearing to risk the pain and bleeding of a disappointed heart. Whether they be battered wives or distraught husbands, some among us have given up—not daring to be transparent with anyone for any reason. These have decided to present a fictitious, fragmented appearance among us that never solidifies or really alters us in any way!

I must admit there is no shield for broken hearts that will protect us from the flaws of those whom we dare to befriend. At best, there will be times of trembling need and emotional debates, yet we need to make the investment and even face the risk of depletion rather than live in a glass bubble all our lives!

Part of Your Destiny

I know that betrayal can be painful. It is hard to receive disloyalty from hands and hearts you trusted. The fear of a "Judas" has caused many preachers, leaders, as well as the general masses to avoid the attack. Now if you understand anything about God, then you know that God can give direction out of rejection. It was Judas' ministry that brought Christ to the cross! Although this betrayal was painful, it was an essential part of His destiny.

It is important to understand destiny as it relates to relationships. God is too wise to have His plans aborted by the petty acts of men. We have to rely on God's divine administration as we become involved with people. Their access to our future is limited by the shield of divine purpose that God Himself has placed on our lives!

I hate double-minded men, but I love Your law. You are my refuge and my shield; I have put my hope in Your word (Psalm 119:113-114 NIV).

The extent of damage that mortals can do to the upright is limited by the purposes of God. What a privilege it is to know that and understand it in your heart. It destroys the constant paranoia that restricts many of us from exploring possible friendships and covenant relationships. Let me be very clear, though; the possibility of getting hurt in a relationship is always present. Any time you make an investment, there is the possibility of a loss. But there is a difference between being hurt and being altered or destroyed.

You belong to God, and He watches over you every day. He monitors your affairs, and acts as your protection. Sometimes He opens doors (we always get excited about God opening doors). But the same God who opens doors also closes doors. I am, perhaps, more grateful for the doors He has closed in my life than I am for the ones He has opened. Had I been allowed to enter some of the doors He closed, I would surely have been destroyed! God doesn't intend for every relationship to flourish. There are some human cliques and social groups in which He doesn't want you to be included!

God Works for Your Good

And to the angel of the church in Philadelphia write, "These things says He who is holy, He who is true, 'He who has the key of David,'" He who opens and no one shuts, and shuts and no one opens (Revelation 3:7).

The letter to the Philadelphia church, the church of brotherly love, basically ends with the words, "I am the One who closes doors." The art to surviving painful moments is living in the "yes" zone. We need to learn to respond to God with a yes when the doors are open, and a yes when they are closed. Our prayer must be:

I trust Your decisions, Lord; and I know that if this relationship is good for me, You will allow it to continue. I know that if the door is closed, then it is also for my good. So I say "yes" to You as I go into this relationship. I appreciate brotherly love, and I still say "yes" if You close the door.

This is the epitome of a trust that is seldom achieved, but is to be greatly sought after. In so doing, you will be able to savor the gift of companionship without the fear of reprisal!

If God allows a relationship to continue, and some negative, painful betrayals come from it, you must realize that He will only allow what ultimately works for your good. Sometimes such a betrayal ushers you into the next level of consecration, a level you could never reach on your own. For that we give thanks! What a privilege to live in the assurance that God is in control of you, and of everyone whom He allows to get behind "the shield" of His purposes for your life!

He intimately knows every person whom He cherishes enough to call His child. Any good parent tries to ensure that his or her children are surrounded by positive influences. The unique thing about God's parenting is that He sometimes uses a negative to bring about a positive. If no good can come out of a relationship or situation, then God will not allow it. This knowledge sets us free from internal struggle and allows us to be transparent.

Every good gift and every perfect gift is from above, and comes down from the Father of lights, with whom there is no variation or shadow of turning (James 1:17).

If you don't understand the sovereignty of God, then all is lost. There must be an inner awareness within your heart, a deep knowledge that God is in control and that He is able to reverse the adverse. When we believe in His sovereignty, we can overcome every humanly induced trial because we realize that they are divinely permitted and supernaturally orchestrated. He orchestrates them in such a way that the things that could have paralyzed us only motivate us.

God delights in bestowing His abundant grace upon us so we can live without fear. In Christ, we come to the table of human relationships feeling like we are standing before a great "smorgasbord" or buffet table. There will be some relationships whose "taste" we prefer over others, but the richness of life is in the opportunity to explore the options. What a dull plate we would face if everything on it was duplicated without distinction. God creates different types of people, and all are His handiwork.

Even in the most harmonious of relationships there are injuries and adversity. If you live in a cocoon, you will miss all the different levels of love God has for you. God allows different people to come into your life to accomplish His purposes. Your friends are ultimately the ones who will help you become all that God wants you to be in Him. When you consider it in that light, you have many friends—some of them expressed friends, and some implied friends.

Judas—A Friend?

Implied friendship describes your relationship with those who weren't consciously or obviously trying to help you, yet their actions—though painful—were ultimately purposeful. Therefore, we glory in tribulation! We now understand that God used their negativity to accomplish His will for our lives. Now, because our ultimate goal is to please Him, we must widen our definition of friendship to include the betrayer if his betrayal ushered us into the next step of God's plan for our lives.

Immediately he went up to Jesus and said, "Greetings, Rabbi!" and kissed Him. But Jesus said to him, "Friend, why have you come?" Then they came and laid hands on

Jesus and took Him. And suddenly, one of those who were with Jesus stretched out his hand and drew his sword, struck the servant of the high priest, and cut off his ear. But Jesus said to him, "Put your sword in its place, for all who take the sword will perish by the sword. Or do you think that I cannot now pray to My Father, and He will provide Me with more than twelve legions of angels? How then could the Scriptures be fulfilled, that it must happen thus?" (Matthew 26:49-54)

I understand that in its narrow sense, a friend is one who has good intentions. However, because of the sovereignty of God, I have come to realize that there are some who were actually instrumental in my blessing, although they never really embraced or affirmed me as a person! They played a crucial part in my well-being. These kinds of "friends" are the "Judas sector" that exists in the life of every child of God.

Every child of God not only has, but also desperately needs, a "Judas" to carry out certain aspects of divine providence in his life! In the passage quoted above, Judas was more of a friend than Peter! Although Peter was certainly more amiable and admirable, Judas was the one God selected to usher in the next step of the process. Peter's love was almost a deterrent to the purpose of God. Sometimes your friends are the ones who can cause you the most pain. They wound you and betray you; but through their betrayal, God's will can be executed in your life.

Judas was no mistake. He was handpicked and selected. His role was crucial to the death and resurrection of Christ. No one helped Christ reach His goal like Judas. If God allowed certain types of people to come into our lives, they would hinder us from His divine purpose.

"Thank You, Lord, for my mysterious friends whose venomous assault led me to lean on You more explicitly than I would have, had they not tried to destroy me!" This is the prayer of the seasoned heart that has been exercised by the tragedies of life. It has reduced and controlled the fatty feelings and emotions that cause us to always seek those whose actions tickle our ears.

We all want to be surrounded by a friend like John, whose loving head lay firmly on Jesus' breast. We may long for the protective instincts of a friend like Peter, who stood ready to attack every negative force that would come against Jesus. In his misdirected love, Peter even withstood Jesus to His face over His determination to die for mankind. But the truth of the matter is, Jesus could have accomplished His goal without Peter, James, or John; but without Judas He would never have reached the hope of His calling!

WHEN YOU ENCOUNTER A JUDAS IN YOUR LIFE, REMEMBER THAT IT IS HIS ACTIONS THAT CARRY OUT THE PURPOSE OF GOD IN YOUR LIFE!

Leave my Judas alone. I need him in my life. He is my mysterious friend, the one who aids me without even knowing it. When you encounter a Judas in your life, remember that it is his actions that carry out the purpose of God in your life! Look back over your life and understand that it is persecution that strengthens you. It is the struggles and the trauma we face that help us persevere.

Thank God for your friends and family and their support, but remember that it is often your relationship with that mysterious friend of malice and strife, weakness and defective behavior, that becomes the catalyst for greatness in your life! It is much easier to forgive the actions of men when you know the purposes of God! Not only should we refuse to fear their actions—we should release them.

What happens when friendship takes an unusual form? Did you know that God, our ultimate Friend, sometimes manipulates the actions of our enemies to cause them to work as friends in order to accomplish His will in our lives? God can bless you through the worst of relationships! That is why we must learn how to accept even the relationships that seem to be painful or negative. The time, effort, and pain we invest in them is not wasted because God knows how to make adversity feed destiny into your life!

THE BLEEDING TRAIL OF BROKEN HEARTS AND WOUNDED RELATIONSHIPS ULTIMATELY LEADS US TO THE RICHNESS OF GOD'S PURPOSE IN US.

In short, the bleeding trail of broken hearts and wounded relationships ultimately leads us to the richness of God's purpose in us. Periodically each of us will hear a knock on the door. It is the knock of our old friend Judas, whose cold kiss and calloused heart usher us into the will of God. To be sure, these betrayals call bloody tears to our eyes and nail us to a cold cross. Nevertheless, the sweet kiss of betrayal can never abort the precious promises of God in our life! The challenge is to sit at the table with Judas on one side and John on the other, and to treat one no differently from the other, even though we are distinctly aware of each one's identity and agenda. If you have been betrayed or wounded by someone you brought too close, please forgive them. He really was a blessing. You will only be better when you cease to be bitter!

It is good for me that I have been afflicted; that I might learn Thy statutes (Psalm 119:71 KJV).

I cannot stop your hurts from coming; neither can I promise that everyone who sits at the table with you is loyal. But I can suggest that the sufferings of success give us direction and build character within us. Finally, as you find the grace to reevaluate your enemies and realize that many of them were friends in disguise, I can only place a warm hand of solace on your sobbing shoulders and wipe the gentle rain of soft tears from your eyes.

As God heals what hurt you have, I want to whisper gently in your ears, "Betrayal is only sweetened when it is accompanied by survival. Live on, my friend, live on—you have the strength to stand!"

Stamina Secrets and Solutions

1. "Only occasionally in the course of a lifetime do we meet the kind of friend that is more than an acquaintance." Are you blessed with a few good friends? Have you thanked God for them recently?

   _____

   _____

   _____

2. You may fear the bitter taste of rejection, but perhaps worse than rejection is the naked pain that attacks an exposed heart when a relationship is challenged by a struggle. Do you easily cast off a friend if a dispute arises?

   _____

   _____

   _____

3. "Your friends are ultimately the ones who will help you become all that God wants you to be in Him. When you consider it in that light, you have many friends—some of them expressed friends, and some implied friends." Have you ever considered your friends in this light? How does it change your attitude toward them?

   _____

   _____

   _____

   _____

4. Jesus could have accomplished His goal without Peter, James, or John; but without Judas, He would never have reached the hope of His calling! Consider how the Judas' in your life helped you accomplish your dreams, calling, and goals.

_____

_____

_____

5. "If you have been betrayed or wounded by someone you brought too close, please forgive him. He really was a blessing. You will only be better when you cease to be bitter!" This may be very difficult to do; pray about it. Then forgive.

_____

_____

_____

CHAPTER 8

Wilderness Before Inheritance

Now Jehoram the son of Ahab began to reign over Israel in Samaria the eighteenth year of Jehoshaphat king of Judah, and reigned twelve years. And he wrought evil in the sight of the LORD; but not like his father, and like his mother: for he put away the image of Baal that his father had made. Nevertheless he cleaved unto the sins of Jeroboam the son of Nebat, which made Israel to sin; he departed not therefrom. And Mesha king of Moab was a sheepmaster, and rendered unto the king of Israel an hundred thousand lambs, and an hundred thousand rams, with the wool. But it came to pass, when Ahab was dead, that the king of Moab rebelled against the king of Israel. And king Jehoram went out of Samaria the same time, and numbered all Israel. And he went and sent to Jehoshaphat the king of Judah, saying, The king of Moab hath rebelled against me: wilt thou go with me against Moab to battle? And he said, I will go up: I am as thou art, my people as thy *people, and my horses as thy horses. And he said, Which way shall we go up? And he answered, The way **through the wilderness** of Edom* (2 Kings 3:1-8 KJV).

When you speak of the wilderness, your mind immediately imagines a dry place where nothing green grows. Everything in the wilderness is brown and unappealing to the eye. The environment of the wilderness is not brightened with any color. Everything in the wilderness has adapted itself to live in this type of climate. Rarely does it rain in the wilderness and when it does, plants store the moisture they need because there is no guarantee when it will rain again.

When we are going through our wilderness experience, we must be like the trees and the other animals of the wilderness. We must learn to adapt our faith to the challenges a wilderness brings.

The animals in the wilderness have learned to travel and hunt at night because it is cooler at night. Spiritually, we too must learn to find a place where the Lord can minister to us in our wilderness. It is a place where He can give us instruction about what to do next. Like the trees that store up water, uncertain of when it will rain again, we must store up His Word in our hearts. Many of us are living in the wilderness for various reasons.

Now it came to pass, as Aaron spoke to the whole congregation of the children of Israel, that they looked toward the wilderness, and behold, the glory of the LORD appeared in the cloud (Exodus 16:10).

The wilderness is a place of dying, where all the things that cause you to stumble in your walk with God are killed. If you have ever watched a movie where people dared to enter the wilderness, with little or no understanding of life in the wilderness, they often did not survive there. Since they had no one to help or advise them, they tried to fight the elements in their own strength.

Likewise, many of us have been in the wilderness and we have tried unsuccessfully to fight the battle in our own strength. You see, the wilderness is a place where God says, "I finally have you in a place where I can speak to you." Because Jehoram was unprepared for life in the wilderness, he needed someone who knew something about the wilderness. Hence, he asked for Jehoshaphat's help.

Do not be fooled into thinking that you can ever be fully prepared for life in the wilderness. Sometimes, God leads us abruptly into the wilderness. He might have been trying to get you to come to Him or to get you to take your spiritual life more seriously. Perhaps He has been trying to draw your attention to the call He has placed in your life.

Then Jesus was led up by the Spirit into the wilderness to be tempted by the devil (Matthew 4:1).

It is indeed a gamble that the Lord takes on us, for He knows that He cannot and will not override our will. But He also knows that it is truly our desire to do His will. Even the worst sinner is inwardly drawn to God even if he does not serve Him.

God loves you so much that He is willing to take just that type of risk on you. He knows that you may either serve Him or reject Him. You may say, "Lord, wherever You lead, I will follow, even through the wilderness." Or you may decide to say, "I can't deal with this. I thought life would be better than this. I quit."

YOU MAY EITHER SERVE HIM OR REJECT HIM.

But God knows that we must be tried in the fire so that we can become as pure as gold. God brings us into the wilderness to perfect our faith. You cannot have all pleasure without pain, neither can you enjoy only good times without adversity. Your faith is perfected in the furnace of affliction and adversity. There is something about going through dilemmas and crises that bring us to the place where we discover things about God which we would not have known under other circumstances.

The sins in Jehoram's life prevented him from walking with God like he should have. His relationship with God was superficial. However, when he got in trouble he needed God as a fire escape. He called on God only when things were going bad. In essence, he wanted to use God as his servant, rather than serve God. He was interested in God only if God served his own selfish purpose.

> *Let nothing be done through selfish ambition or conceit, but in lowliness of mind let each esteem others better than himself* (Philippians 2:3).

Many of us have tried to use God for personal gain. We view God as a spiritual Santa Claus who is there at our every whim, one who will bring us gifts and presents that are beyond our reach. The only time we talk with Him is when we need something from Him.

If a loved one becomes terminally ill, we immediately call on Him. We are ready to beat down the pastor's door so that he can pray for us, or we call on the saints and implore their spiritual prayer and support. But, for some, as soon as the problem is over, what happens? We slump right back into the backslidden state we were in before the problem jolted us to pray. That is why many of us are constantly in problems.

> *And when you pray, you shall not be like the hypocrites. For they love to pray standing in the synagogues and on the corners of the streets, that they may be seen by men. Assuredly, I say to you, they have their reward* (Matthew 6:5).

God is fully aware of the sad fact that should we have all our needs met, we will never seek Him with all our hearts. Like the children of Israel, we tend to become arrogant and prideful, and forget the fact that we must fully acknowledge God in times of prosperity as well as adversity.

Jehoram was pretty smart, and he knew something about God. Realizing that he did not have a sound relationship with the Lord, he courted the friendship of one who did. He said to Jehoshaphat, king of Judah, "I have got to go out to fight and I want you to fight with me."

Jehoshaphat replied, "If you are going to war, I will go with you. My people are your people. I'm going to assume the responsibility of getting you the victory and all my captains and all my warriors are at your disposal." The next question was how to go about it.

SEEK GOD'S MIND ON THE MATTER.

They had to seek the mind of God on the matter. One of the servants of the king of Israel told Jehoshaphat about Elisha who had the word of the Lord. Jehoshaphat, Jehoram, and the king of Edom therefore traveled to see Elisha, the prophet.

> *And Elisha said unto the king of Israel, What have I to do with thee? get thee to the prophets of thy father, and to the prophets of thy mother....As the LORD of hosts liveth, before whom I stand, surely, were it not that I regard the presence of Jehoshaphat the king of Judah, I would not look toward thee, nor see thee* (2 Kings 3:13-14 KJV).

Sometimes we are so obsessed with our destination that we forget we must go through various phases to get there. For example, when a woman is pregnant, it is apparent to all that she is carrying a baby. After the baby is born, all we see is a beautiful baby. We forget that there is a process of bringing that baby into the world—a process that is painful for both the mother and the child.

For the mother, it is the process of pushing this new delicate life out of her body where it has lived snugly for nine long, peaceful months. For the baby, it is the process of being pushed into a place that it perceives to be unfriendly and cold, very different from the home it had occupied for nine months.

> *For whatever is born of God overcomes the world. And this is the **victory** that has overcome the world—our faith* (1 John 5:4).

Just like the baby in the mother's womb, we may have to let go of something that has become part of us. We are always confessing that we want the perfect will of God for our lives, but we must not forget the fact that we must conquer the obstacles that stand in the way of our future success in which God's ultimate will is realized.

King Jehoshaphat asked the question, "How shall we go up against Moab to get victory?" The unexpected answer was, "You have to go through the wilderness of Edom to get the victory" (see 2 Kings 3:8).

My friend, if you want to get the victory, you must be willing to go through the wilderness. I want to reiterate this fact: it is not always easy to get the victory because it belongs to the other side of the wilderness. You must be willing to *go through* a little time of abasement, confusion, adversity, and even opposition before you arrive at your destination.

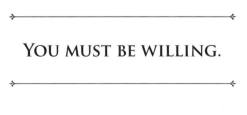

YOU MUST BE WILLING.

Many may think that it is unfair to go through this phase. But you see, it is the wilderness that weeds out the saints from the "aint's." It is the wilderness that weeds out people who really want to do something for God from people who just have a momentary, superficial, mundane relationship with Him. It is the wilderness that makes a hypocrite back up and say, "I can't take it anymore."

The wilderness, God's killing field, will weed out all the impostors because they cannot survive the adversity of the wilderness. The wilderness weeds out the saints from the "ain'ts."

I want to warn you that you will have to go through the wilderness to attain the will of God for your life. The wilderness teaches us to stand; it teaches us to cast our cares upon Him. It teaches us to rely and totally depend on Him for life support, because we know in due season we shall reap if we faint not.

He shall be like a tree planted by the rivers of water, that brings forth its fruit in its season, whose leaf also shall not wither; and whatever he does shall prosper (Psalm 1:3).

Some of us cannot handle the smallest problems. We feel that the hardships placed on our path indicate that God either has forsaken us or is punishing us for some sin we have committed. The devil has successfully employed that lie to deter us from seeking the heavenly Father. Do not for a moment think that you can do it on your own. You will fail woefully.

Remember Joshua and Caleb. Had they tried to enter the Promised Land on their own strength or cognizance, they would have perished in the wilderness. Even when life in the wilderness became dull and unappealing, they did not stop seeking God; neither did they cease to rely on His guidance. Like Joshua and Caleb, we must be persistent in faith even in the wilderness where problems are at their peak.

"Surely none of the men who came up from Egypt, from twenty years old and above, shall see the land of which I

*swore to Abraham, Isaac, and Jacob, because they have not wholly followed Me, **except Caleb** the son of Jephunneh, the Kenizzite, and **Joshua** the son of Nun, **for they have wholly followed the** LORD." So the* LORD's *anger was aroused against Israel, and He made them wander in the wilderness forty years, until all the generation that had done evil in the sight of the* LORD *was gone* (Numbers 32:11-13).

The greatest battle that we face while we are in the wilderness is the one between the new and the old man. The old man that God is trying to kill in the wilderness refuses to die. It wants to resurrect old hurts and old problems. But, as new creatures in Christ Jesus, we must put the old man to death.

*That you **put off,** concerning your former conduct, the **old man** which grows corrupt according to the deceitful lusts, and **be renewed** in the spirit of your mind, and that you put on the **new man** which was created according to God, in true righteousness and holiness* (Ephesians 4:22-25).

Despite the situations you are facing, you must constantly remind yourself that you are a new creature and the old man is dead!

Stamina Secrets and Solutions

1. Have you learned to adapt your faith to the challenges a wilderness brings? Think of five ways to change your mindset and/or lifestyle to ensure victory.

_____

_____

_____

_____

_____

2. "Spiritually, we too must learn to find a place where the Lord can minister to us in our wilderness. It is a place where He can give us instruction about what to do next." Have you found this special place? If not, actively search for it and claim it.

_____

_____

_____

3. If you want victory, you must be willing to go through the wilderness. How willing are you to walk through the wilderness? Your attitude and trust in God make all the difference.

_____

_____

_____

4. The wilderness, God's killing field, weeds out all the impostors because they cannot survive the adversity of the wilderness. You are not an impostor—you are a child of God, strong and true to His calling. Claim this fact today.

_____

_____

_____

5. The greatest battle that you face while in the wilderness is the one between the new you and the old you. Concentrate on the new you and focus on all the blessings afforded you as His heir.

_____

_____

_____

CHAPTER 9

Healing for Past Hurts

The steps of a good man are ordered by the
LORD, and He delights in his way. Though he fall,
he shall not be utterly cast down: for ***the LORD***
upholds him *with His hand* (Psalm 37:23-24).

Has something so painful and overwhelming happened to you that it has affected every area of your life? Every time you kneel to pray, does your mind go back to the fact that someone broke your heart and wounded your spirit?

Have you experienced something so personally devastating that you can't discuss it with anyone? You find it difficult to trust people, and you don't know where to turn. You may feel as if everyone is grading you and evaluating your progress—when actually you are your own harshest judge.

You know you should be further along in life, but someone or some circumstance crippled your faith. Your hopes and dreams were never fulfilled.

You know you should have finished school; you know you should have been a teacher or a musician by now. By society's standards, you should already be married and have children.

Maybe you think your ministry should be further along or that you should have a successful career at this point in your life. Your dreams and goals should have been fulfilled years ago, but you've been crippled.

Don't give up. There is hope for you and healing for past hurts.

Dreams Fulfilled

Joseph had dreams. It took years, however, for those dreams to be fulfilled. In spite of the tragedies in his life, Joseph never let go of the dreams God had given him.

Now Israel loved Joseph more than all his children, because he was the son of his old age. Also he made him a tunic [coat] of many colors. But when his brothers saw that their father loved him more than all his brothers, they hated him and could not speak peaceably to him. Now Joseph had a dream, and he told it to his brothers; and they hated him even more (Genesis 37:3-5).

On the outside, Joseph was a have-not, rejected, and despised by his own brothers. God had plans for Joseph long before he was ever sold into slavery. From the circumstances, however, that fact didn't always appear to be true. Nevertheless, God had His hand on Joseph's life.

While in slavery and in prison, Joseph was not experiencing conditions that indicated he was going to be successful. He didn't look like a man marked to be a great leader, but he was.

And the LORD was with Joseph, and he was a prosperous man; and he was in the house of his master the Egyptian. And his master saw that the LORD was with him, and that the LORD made all that he did to prosper in his hand. ... The keeper of the prison looked not to any thing that was under his hand; because the LORD was with him, and that which he did, the LORD *made it to prosper* (Genesis 39:2-3,23 KJV).

God, however, has a way of taking people who have been forsaken by others and raising them up. In fact, God tends to prefer such individuals because, when they get into a place of power, they are not arrogant like those who think they deserve to be promoted.

Egypt's Pharaoh recognized these qualities in Joseph and exalted him to the highest position in the nation.

And Pharaoh said to his servants, "Can we find such a one as this, a man in whom is the Spirit of God?" Then Pharaoh said to Joseph, "Inasmuch as God has shown you all this, there is no one as discerning and wise as you. You shall be over my house, and all my people shall be ruled according to your word; only in regard to the throne will I be greater than you." And Pharaoh said to Joseph, "See, I have set you over all the land of Egypt" (Genesis 41:38-41).

Broken individuals tend not to be quite so self-righteous. They tend to be a little warmer and more loving, reaching out to embrace others without fear of rejection. They understand that if it had not been for the Lord, they wouldn't be who they are. They realize that if it had not been for God's grace and mercy, they would have never survived.

Joseph exhibited these qualities in the way he treated his once-hateful brothers. When he revealed himself, instead of condemning them for their act of violence against him, Joseph forgave his brothers.

And Joseph said to his brothers, "Please come near to me." So they came near. Then he said: "I am Joseph your brother, whom you sold into Egypt. But now, do not therefore be grieved or angry with yourselves because you sold me here; for God sent me before you to preserve life. For these two years the famine has been in the land, and there are still five years in which there will be neither plowing nor harvesting. And God sent me before you to preserve a posterity for you in the earth, and to save your lives by a great deliverance. So now it was not you who sent me here, but God; and He has made me a father to Pharaoh, and lord of all his house, and a ruler throughout all the land of Egypt (Genesis 45:4-8).

Joseph did not blame God for his former troubles, instead he realized that God's hand had been on his life all along.

Healed to Help Others

God has a way of bringing us out of bondage and then making us remember where we came from. When we—like Joseph—begin to experience success and victory, God will remind us that He opened the door of the prison. He set us free. He gave us favor in the eyes of men. Now it is our turn to bless others. When God raises you up, you'll have more compassion for other people. You'll look for people you can help.

Then the King will say to those on His right hand, "Come, you blessed of My Father, inherit the kingdom prepared for you from the foundation of the world: for I was hungry and you gave Me food; I was thirsty and you gave Me drink; I was a stranger and you took Me in; I was naked and you clothed Me; I was sick and you visited Me; I was in prison and you came to Me." Then the righteous will answer Him, saying, "Lord, when did we see You hungry and feed You, or thirsty and give You drink? When did we see You a stranger and take You in, or naked and clothe You? Or when did we see You sick, or in prison, and come to You?" And the King will answer and say to them, "Assuredly, I say to you, inasmuch as you did it to one of the least of these My brethren, you did it to Me" (Matthew 25:34-40).

The church needs healed and delivered Christians who are willing to be used by God to bless others. God is looking for people who have enough compassion to stop and ask, "How are you today?" and then stay long enough to hear the answer.

Instead of always expecting someone to bless you, be moved to help a brother or sister in need. It was God's grace and mercy that allowed you to survive the situation that crippled you. Now it is your responsibility to remember and encourage those who may be experiencing a similar problem.

*A new commandment I give to you, that you **love one** **another**; as I have loved you, that you also **love one another*** (John 13:34).

When people have been wounded and crippled by the circumstances of life, they need special care, extra attention, and unconditional love. They have to be held a little closer and prayed over a little longer because their trust has been broken and betrayed.

They may have been told by well-meaning friends, "I'm going to be there for you." Others have said, "You can depend one me." But they lied.

I know pastors who trusted and depended on fellow associates only to be betrayed and stabbed in the back. Now these pastors are crippled and unable to minister.

I also know church people who have been disillusioned by pastors who used them and then discarded them like an old worn-out shirt. As a result, these wounded workers walk with a limp, crippled by unforgiveness and fear.

NO ONE IS EXEMPT FROM BEING CRIPPLED, BUT EVERYONE CAN BE HEALED.

No one is exempt from being crippled, but everyone can be healed if they allow the Lord to shoulder all of their past hurts and tear down the walls of unforgiveness. Unforgiveness is a stronghold that sets up residence in the heart. It causes you to be hard-hearted, angry, and bitter toward others and even toward God!

> *And whenever you stand praying, if you have anything against anyone, **forgive** him, that your Father in heaven may also **forgive** you your trespasses* (Mark 11:25).

If you forgive those who have hurt you, the Holy Spirit can bring healing. He will come to you and say, "You are hurting, but you're going to make it. You've been wounded, but I'm going to help you. I know you've got a weak side, but I'm going to strengthen you. I know you don't have a lot of help, but I'm going to be your support. I know you have been abandoned, but I'm going to stand by you."

What Only *You* Can Do

You may have asked "How can a perfect God have a crippled child?" God specializes in taking those who have been broken and neglected by others and restoring them. God says, "I take little and create much."

You have more potential than you think. You can achieve much more than people expect of you. You can go as far in life as your faith will take you.

They said you won't last, but He can strengthen you. They said God could not use someone like you, but He thinks differently. God sees potential that not even you know is there.

You may be saying to yourself, *I've done so much wrong, I can't get up; I'm so far out that I can't get back in.*

THE DEVIL IS A LIAR!

The devil is a liar! It does not matter what you have done. It does not matter where you have been. God is a God of second chances. He is the God of new beginnings. When you're down, He'll pick you up again.

When God restores you, it does not matter who is trying to bind you or who is fighting against you. All you need to know is that when God brings you up, no demon in hell can bring you down.

If God has blessed you, shout it from the housetops! If God brought you up, praise and thank Him! Every time I think about what the Lord has done for me, my soul rejoices.

Now it came to pass, afterward, that He went through every city and village, preaching and bringing the glad tidings of the kingdom of God. And the twelve were with Him, and certain women who had been healed of evil spirits and infirmities—Mary called Magdalene, out of whom had come seven demons (Luke 8:1-2).

No one can tell your testimony. No one knows what God has done for you. No one knows how far you've come. No one knows what you've been through. But you know it was only by the grace of God that you survived. Don't allow the devil to steal your testimony.

It may have taken you longer than everybody else, but God has given you the victory. Tell others what God has done in your life. The devil would love for you not to tell your testimony. Why? Because if you tell what God has done for you, someone else might get set free.

God's Mercy

There is not a person alive today who has not benefited from God's mercy. It was God's mercy that prevailed in the Garden of Eden. When Adam and Eve sinned, the Lord could have scrapped everything and started all over again. God was merciful and allowed Adam and Eve to live with the hope that their seed would redeem back what they had lost.

GOD'S MERCY PREVAILS.

God's mercy prevailed in the wilderness with Moses and the children of Israel. When the Israelites moaned and groaned, their fate could have ended in immediate and total destruction, but God was merciful.

When Jonah refused to go to Nineveh, God could have killed the unwilling prophet and found another to go in his place. It was God's mercy that allowed the fish to swallow Jonah. God knew what was in Jonah just as He knows what is in you and me.

Sometimes God will allow us to fall because in our time of falling we come to realize that without Him we are nothing. We become convinced that it is only by His mercy that we are able to stand.

"His mercy endureth for ever. Let the redeemed of the LORD say so" (Ps. 107:1b-2a KJV). These verses remind us of the song, "Your Grace and Mercy," which simply says:

> *Your grace and mercy has*
> *brought me through,*
> *And I'm living this moment*
> *because of You.*

I want to thank You and
praise You, too;
Your grace and mercy has
brought me through.

God's grace and mercy has brought you through. Quit acting as if you have made it on your own. Stop pretending you're here because you're so good. The devil is a liar, and he would have you deceived into thinking your deliverance was and is by some act or power of your own.

O give thanks unto the LORD, for He is good: for His mercy endureth for ever (Psalm 107:1 KJV).

God's Sufficient Grace

The apostle Paul wrote, *"And He said unto me, My grace is sufficient for thee: for **my strength is made perfect in weakness"** (2 Cor. 12:9 KJV).

When we are asking and believing God for something, it may take time for it to become a reality in our lives. As a result, the spirit of discouragement attempts to latch onto us and drag us down, saying, "You're not going to get it. You're not going to get up. You're not going to be free. You're not going to get out. You're not going to be loosed. You're not going to be happy, and you're not going to have joy. You're not ever going to be satisfied. You're going to die frustrated. You're going to end up depressed and discouraged."

The devil is a liar. He wants us to think there is no help in God and no balm in Gilead. God may not come when you want Him to come, but He's always right on time—if you wait on Him.

For the LORD God is a sun and shield; the LORD will give grace and glory; no good thing will He withhold from those who walk uprightly (Psalm 84:11).

Whatever God declares or decrees, He has the power to perform. He has never yet said anything that He couldn't back up. He has never claimed to be able to do anything that He could not do.

Never be in a position where you are too good or too busy to ask God for help. Never get to a point where you think you can make it on your own. That is pride at its worst. And before a fall there is pride, and after pride there is destruction.

Without God's help, we would all be doomed to lives of pain and self-destruction. When I have been desperate and afflicted, I knew it was the power of the Holy Spirit that carried me and rescued me.

THE POWER OF THE HOLY SPIRIT GIVES YOU STRENGTH TO STAND.

We cannot do anything without God. We can't breathe without God. We can't think without God. We can't even get up without God.

Don't let satan deceive you into believing that you can make it on your own. As soon as you fall, satan is right there whispering, "You will never get up."

But you can call on God for help and realize that He is always *"near at hand…and not a God afar off"* (Jer. 23:23).

Stamina Secrets and Solutions

1. "Has something so painful and overwhelming happened to you that it has affected every area of your life?" You can take comfort in the fact that God is greater than any lie satan keeps telling you. You *can* overcome every pain and past hurt.

   _____

   _____

   _____

   _____

2. Unforgiveness is a stronghold that sets up residence in your heart. With the strength of the Holy Spirit within you— give unforgiveness an eviction notice today.

   _____

   _____

   _____

3. When God brings you up, no demon in hell can bring you down. When you have been delivered, share your story with others. Everyone needs to hear the message of hope.

   _____

   _____

   _____

   _____

4. God knew what was in Jonah just as He knows what is in
   you. Dare to believe the best about yourself—God does.

   _____

   _____

   _____

5. Without God's help, you would be doomed to live a life
   of pain and self-destruction. Thank God, and praise Him
   as often as possible, throughout each day, for His tender
   mercy.

   _____

   _____

   _____

CHAPTER 10

Getting Back on Track

*Therefore let him who thinks he stands take heed
lest he fall* (1 Corinthians 10:12).

You may have heard the story about the misbehaving little boy whose mother told him to sit in the corner chair. "I may be sitting on the outside," he said, "but I'm standing on the inside."

That's the way many adults act when they rebel against God. Standing in our own strength, however, puts us most in danger of falling. When we think we are strong, we are easy prey for the devil.

Between the Devil and the Deep Blue Sea

The prophet Jonah did not want to do what he knew he was called to do. Instead, he murmured and complained and then tried to run. We can't run from God, but we can run out from under the protection of the Lord.

STANDING IN YOUR OWN STRENGTH
PUTS YOU IN DANGER OF FALLING.

That is what Jonah did, but God didn't stop chasing him. He caused a fish to swallow him.

While in the belly of the great fish, Jonah said, "I've messed up. I've blown it. I've goofed. I've gotten into trouble. I've gotten myself in a mess." Jonah realized he had fallen, and he was now in a place where he had to repent of his rebellion.

> *Then Jonah prayed to the LORD his God from the fish's belly. And he said: "I cried out to the LORD because of my affliction, and He answered me. Out of the belly of Sheol I cried, and You heard my voice. For You cast me into the deep, into the heart of the seas, and the floods surrounded me; all Your billows and Your waves passed over me. Then I said, 'I have been cast out of Your sight; yet I will look again toward Your holy temple'"* (Jonah 2:1-4).

Notice how Jonah's emotions wavered. At one moment, Jonah was calling on God, but then doubt rose up in his heart and he said, "I am cast out of God's sight."

Has the devil ever told you, "God is not even thinking about you; God can't see you; God doesn't love you anymore; He doesn't care about you; after all, you sinned"?

In the midst of Jonah's feeble prayer, the thought popped up: "I'm too far gone, and I'm cast out of His sight."

Have you ever had to pray with fear in your heart and uncertainty in your spirit not knowing in your own mind whether God could hear you or not?

God is not deaf, nor is He hard of hearing. God is not like Grandpa; He's God. He can hear your thoughts afar off. He can hear a snake moving through the grass in the middle of a rain storm. He knows what you are trying to say even before you say it.

Therefore submit to God. Resist the devil and he will flee from you. Draw near to God and He will draw near to you... (James 4:7-8).

God will raise you up if you ask Him. Like Jonah, you don't have to do anything special to get God's attention. All He asks is that you humble yourself. God wants you to be delivered out of your desperate situation, but it is up to you not to resist the Holy Ghost. Submit humbly to God; resist the devil and the devil will flee from you. First, you must submit—as Jonah did—to God and His will for your life.

Going Around in Circles

It takes more than just saying you submit to God. You have to walk it out day by day trusting Him to lead and guide you into deliverance and fulfillment. If you don't, you will only end up going around in circles.

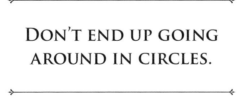

DON'T END UP GOING AROUND IN CIRCLES.

After the children of Israel were freed from Egyptian bondage, they spent the majority of their time complaining about their circumstances. Rather than thanking God for His miraculous deliverance, they murmured and griped constantly about their living conditions.

As a result, an 11-day journey to Canaan took 40 years. The children of Israel wandered around in the wilderness until all of the original complainers died off.

They forgot God their Savior, who had done great things in Egypt, wondrous works in the land of Ham, awesome things by the Red Sea. Therefore He said that He would destroy them, had not Moses His chosen one stood before Him in the breach, to turn away His wrath, lest He destroy them. Then they despised the pleasant land; they did not believe His word, but complained in their tents, and did not heed the voice of the LORD. Therefore He raised His hand in an oath against them, to overthrow them in the wilderness, to overthrow their descendants among the nations, and to scatter them in the lands (Psalm 106:21-27).

The doubters and complainers could not enter into God's place of peace and tranquility because of unbelief.

God had tolerated, as long as He could, the people's ungratefulness to Him for bringing them out of 400 years of hard, cruel Egyptian slavery and bondage. God had taken all He was going to of their whining and crying, like little spoiled babies, because they couldn't get their way.

He fed them meals day and night; He provided them with free lights—the sun by day and a pillar of fire by night. God put clothes on their backs and shoes on their feet, neither of which ever wore out or grew old. But through all of this, they were not content and failed to show or express to God any gratitude or thankfulness. All they did was complain, complain, and complain.

Frustrating God's Grace

The Israelites' grumbling and complaining was not what finally frustrated God's tolerance. Their immature behavior simply exemplified the condition of their hearts.

What really displeased God was their failure to walk by faith—their evil hearts of unbelief. *"Take heed, brethren, lest there be in any of you an evil heart of unbelief, in departing from the living God"* (Heb. 3:12 KJV). A hard heart provokes God more than anything else.

> *While it is said, Today if ye will hear His voice, harden not your hearts, as in the provocation. For some, when they had heard, did provoke: howbeit not all that came out of Egypt by Moses. But with whom was He grieved forty years? Was it not with them that had sinned, whose carcases fell in the wilderness? And to whom sware He that they should not enter into His rest, but to them that believed not?* (Hebrews 3:15-18 KJV)

When you do not trust in God's goodness and walk in unbelief, you frustrate the generous grace of God. The apostle Paul wrote, *"I do not frustrate the grace of God: for if righteousness comes by the law, then Christ is dead in vain"* (Gal. 2:21 KJV).

I warn you, brother and sister, do not frustrate the grace of God as the Israelites did. The Bible says that God will not always strive with man. God is merciful, longsuffering, and forgiving, but that does not absolve or excuse us from yielding to the Spirit so that we may be empowered to take responsibility for our own salvation.

> *Therefore, my beloved, as you have always obeyed, not as in my presence only, but now much more in my absence, work out your own salvation with fear and trembling; for **it is God** who works in you both to will and to do for His good pleasure* (Philippians 2:12-13).

We are without excuse, for God has given us everything we need for eternal life and godliness. Why insist on doing things your own way? Submit to God and He will give you the power to overcome every obstacle in your life, one by one.

Religion can't help you. Trying to abide by legalistic church traditions won't help you out of your situation. The only Source guaranteed to pull you through, every time you ask, is God Almighty.

Our Heavenly Defense Attorney

What was God's purpose for taking the Israelites through the wilderness pathway? He wanted to develop their faith in His goodness and in His ability and willingness to help them. God wanted them to know that He would care for and protect them and meet their every need regardless of the circumstances or the situations at hand.

They failed to get the picture. As a result, many were destroyed by snake bites, earthquakes, and various plagues. God would have killed them all; but Moses, who was the friend of God, gained a reprieve by pleading their case before God.

We no longer have Moses today, but as born-again citizens of the Kingdom of God, we have an Advocate who sits at the right hand of the Father constantly making intercession for the saints of Almighty God. His name is Jesus.

> *Wherefore He is able also to save them to the uttermost that come unto God by Him, seeing He ever liveth to make intercession for them* (Hebrews 7:25 KJV).

Before God will let you go under, He will take you over. In the meantime, you will experience "struggling time." Your faith has to be tried. And when your faith is being tested, all hell breaks loose.

During times of tribulation, demons begin to attack your faith. Satan brings false accusations against you during the trial of your faith. Principalities bring condemning indictments, but you cannot lose with the Lawyer I use. Jesus has never lost a case.

The Word of God declares, *"If we say that we have not sinned, we make Him a liar, and His word is not in us"* (1 John 1:10). But the

Word of God also goes on to say that if anyone does sin, *"we have an Advocate with the Father, Jesus Christ the righteous"* (1 John 2:1b).

Jesus Christ is our constant Advocate and our High Priest before God:

> *Seeing then that we have a great High Priest who has passed through the heavens, Jesus the Son of God, let us hold fast our confession. For we do not have a High Priest who cannot sympathize with our weaknesses, but was in all points tempted as we are, yet without sin* (Hebrews 4:14-15).

Do not allow your situation to lock you into a spirit of delusion and complacency. Remember, the devil is trying to kill you. He wants you dead. Only the Spirit of God and the blood of Jesus stand between you and destruction. Do not let satan deceive you into thinking that no one cares or that God has not heard your cries for help.

God knows your moanings and your groanings. God knows what your tears mean when they well up in your eyes. If you call on Him, He will answer you. Trust Him. If He said He will bring you through, He will.

TRUST HIM.

Quit complaining about your situation. Ask God to help you, put away your pride and just ask for help. Do not allow pride to keep you immobilized in your fallen state.

Something in you has got to cry, "Lord, help! I've fallen, and I can't get up! I don't like the way I'm living; I don't like the way I'm hurting. Something in me needs to change. Something in me needs to be broken. I need to be set free by the power of God."

All you have to do is ask. God says:

Ask, and it will be given to you; seek, and you will find; knock, and it will be opened to you (Matthew 7:7).

Remember, you have a High Priest who has made it possible for you to come boldly before the throne of grace to seek help in your time of need. When you seek God with your whole heart, you will find Him.

Stamina Secrets and Solutions

1. "I may be sitting on the outside," he said, "but I'm standing on the inside." Have you ever used this attitude when God tells you to do something? How rebellious are you concerning God's destiny for your life?

_____

_____

_____

_____

2. "Jonah realized he had fallen, and he was now in a place where he had to repent of his rebellion." Although you may not be in the belly of a whale, where has rebellion held you hostage over the years? Now?

_____

_____

_____

_____

3. Complainers can't enter into God's place of peace and tranquility. If you are feeling confusion and turmoil, have you been complaining?

_____

_____

_____

4. Yielding to the Spirit means you will be empowered to take responsibility for your own salvation. You will have the strength to stand if you yield to the Holy Spirit.

_____

_____

_____

5. If God knows what your tears mean when they well up in your eyes, why turn to anyone else for comfort?

_____

_____

_____

_____

CHAPTER 11

Power of Praise and Intimacy in Worship

I will bless the LORD at all times: His praise shall continually be in my mouth. My soul shall make its boast in the LORD; the humble shall hear of it, and be glad. O magnify the LORD with me, and let us exalt His name together. I sought the LORD, and He heard me, and delivered me from all my fears. They looked to Him and were radiant and their faces were not ashamed (Psalm 34:1-5).

Praise is magnifying and exalting the Lord in our hearts. Praise is glorifying the Lord with the fruit of our lips. When we begin to praise God with all our heart, we lose sight of the magnitude of our problems as we gain a vision of the greatness of our Lord.

In order to truly praise God, we must learn to go beyond ourselves and our human limitations. Many times when the enemies of Israel encamped around them, God told Joshua to send out the tribe of Judah first. Judah means praise. Judah marched before the enemies of Israel, armed with nothing but instruments of praise.

PRAISE IS MAGNIFYING AND EXALTING THE LORD IN OUR HEARTS.

When the tribe of Judah began to praise God with their whole heart, God set ambushes among the enemy and confused them. The same principle happens in the spirit realm. When we really begin to praise God, our praise confounds the enemy, and demonic forces begin to withdraw their power and influence.

> *For though we walk in the flesh, we do not war according to the flesh: For the weapons of our warfare are not carnal but mighty in God for pulling down strongholds, casting down arguments and every high thing that exalts itself against the knowledge of God, bringing every thought into captivity to the obedience of Christ* (2 Corinthians 10:3-5).

Praise and worship is the most profound way of expressing our love to the Father. God loves to be praised and worshiped. However, in order to praise God, we must understand the power that praise and worship wield. Praise and worship can break demonic strongholds that have bound us.

Praise and the Word of God are able to pull down strongholds. There is power in praise and worship. Let us pause here to examine this concept of praise as a weapon against spiritual strongholds.

PRAISE AND WORSHIP CAN BREAK DEMONIC STRONGHOLDS.

First, let us define strongholds. Strongholds are roadblocks or stumbling blocks that prevent God's people from truly releasing themselves in praise and worship to God. There are many strongholds, but we will only talk about a couple of them.

The erection of strongholds take place in our thought process.

For example, suppose you were visiting a new church where their method of praise and worship is somewhat different from yours. Immediately, your mind tells you that their way is wrong, or, worse still, that they are not saved. This is a stronghold. Remember that a stronghold is a belief system that is contrary to what God's Word says. You see, in this case, your church has spoken against being too expressive in worship and praise. To them praise and worship does not have to be loud and noisy.

Then David and all the house of Israel played music before the LORD on all kinds of instruments of fir wood, on harps, on stringed instruments, on tambourines, on sistrums, and on cymbals (2 Samuel 6:5).

I have noticed that many people in the church do not know how to worship or praise the Father. We get nervous when someone during service gets too loud and starts to worship God differently from our normal style. We want to worship God in low voices, and that's only on Sunday mornings in our lofty buildings. We must appear "respectable." But in the clubs, or at baseball and football games, the same people will yell and make as much noise as they can without getting the least bit nervous or losing their "respectability."

The Lord loves to hear us praise His holy name and doesn't get nervous when we either become too loud or too quiet. It is we who discriminate about how to praise God. We must be very cautious about this area of our lives. If we allow satan to build up strongholds, we create more roadblocks in our minds that prevent us from praising God freely. Someone once said, "A free person is a dangerous person because he does not allow anyone to dictate what he says or does except the Lord!"

It is good that one should hope and wait quietly for the salvation of the LORD (Lamentations 3:26).

Once the believers understand how satan uses strongholds to keep them from releasing themselves in praise and worship, they are better prepared to use their weapons of praise and worship. Someone once said, "We must understand that the area of thought is both the first and final battlefield. It begins with the mind before it goes to any other area." Hence, satan fights us in our minds to such great extent.

What Is Praise?

Praise is replacing your thoughts and the enemy's thoughts with the thoughts of God. The Word of God, the name of Jesus, and the blood of Jesus are weapons of God that transform and change our thoughts. Although many people may not realize this truth, a tremendous amount of power is released when praise is offered to God. All too often we take this weapon for granted. Imagine what David felt as he composed his psalms. When you take God's thoughts and enter into praise, you become like a battering ram against the strongholds that satan has erected in your mind.

And now my head shall be lifted up above my enemies all around me; therefore I will offer sacrifices of joy in His tabernacle; I will sing, yes, I will sing praises to the LORD (Psalm 27:6).

To the end that my glory may sing praise to You and not be silent. O LORD my God, I will give thanks to You forever (Psalm 30:12).

To You, O my Strength, I will sing praises; for God is my defense, My God of mercy (Psalm 59:17).

Enter into His gates with thanksgiving, and into His courts with praise. Be thankful to Him, and bless His name (Psalm 100:4).

From the rising of the sun to its going down the LORD's name is to be praised (Psalm 113:3).

Another stronghold that we must pull down is the idea that the believer should look sad and gloomy whenever he is going through a difficult time. We think that the devil is having his heyday with us, using us like a dust rag. This ought not to be. We must speak God's Word over the state of our emotions. It is indeed possible to change the state of your mind through the Word of God. Satan tries to destroy you through your mind. Allow the Lord to direct you.

Have you ever heard the voice of God through the thick of the night and thereby you get your victory? It wasn't because you were smart; it wasn't because you were taught; it wasn't because you were so good, but it came just because you learned to say, "Lord, I love You, I praise You. I'm in trouble, but I still love You. I have trials, but I still love You. I don't feel well this morning, but I still love You. I have bills I can't pay, but I still love You." David said, *"I will bless the LORD at all times"* (Ps. 34:1).

Music and Praise

"But now bring me a musician." Then it happened, when the musician played, that the hand of the LORD came upon him (2 Kings 3:15).

In this Scripture, Elisha requested a musician because he saw the need for music. We too need some music in the church. Music can change attitudes and emotions within us. It has the ability to mold and shape thoughts. We have an assortment of instruments—drums, tambourines, organs, and pianos. One king obtained the victory just because he had an orchestra with him. The musicians of the temple of the Lord played musical instruments until the enemy of Israel became confused and started killing one another.

God loves music. He said, "If you want Me to move, play Me some music. Get Me somebody who has an instrument." When Saul was possessed with demons, David played his harp until the demons left Saul. There is something about the anointed music of the Holy Spirit.

And so it was, whenever the spirit from God was upon Saul, that David would take a harp and play it with his hand. Then Saul would become refreshed and well, and the distressing spirit would depart from him (1 Samuel 16:23).

Anointed music will drive out demons, trouble, and sickness. That is why you must be very careful about the type of music that you allow to enter your soul for it has a great effect on your inner man (spirit man). Get some anointed and powerful music. If you want your body to be healed, get some music that speaks healing into your body. Elisha said, "Get me somebody who will play me a song." The Bible says that when the minstrel began to play, the Word of the Lord began to flow out of Elisha's mouth.

Don't you allow anyone to take your song from your lips. You may lose friends, but don't lose your song. You might not sing well in the hearing of other people, but keep your song. You might croak like a frog, but keep your song. David said, *"Make a joyful noise unto God, all ye lands"* (Ps. 66:1 KJV).

Paul demonstrated that if you have a song, you can sing your way out of the jail. If you have a song, you can encourage yourself. Even when there is nobody around to encourage you, and you feel all alone, if you have a song you can encourage yourself in the Lord.

The LORD *is my strength and song, and He has become my salvation; He is my God, and I will praise Him; My father's God, and I will exalt Him* (Exodus 15:2).

God will move when you start praising Him. When you start to praise God, He will come in the middle of your drought, in the middle of your wilderness, and in the middle of your dry place, and say, "I've got a plan!"

Intimacy in Worship

You shall worship the LORD *your God, and Him only you shall serve* (Matthew 4:10).

Whatever we worship is what we ultimately will end up serving. Our nature demands that we worship something. What we worship is up to us.

But the hour is coming, and now is, when the true worshipers will worship the Father in spirit and truth: for the Father is seeking such to worship Him (John 4:23).

To experience true worship you must first develop a relationship with the Father. All relationships are dependent upon good communication. For us as believers, prayer is the means of communicating with the Father. This relationship can be likened to that of a man and his wife. There is the sense of intimacy, closeness, and oneness. It is the closeness that you should never share with anyone else.

When a man and a woman first get married, their relationship is new and exists on that level of looking deeply into each other's eyes. This is the honeymoon stage. At this stage, each worships the ground that the other walks on. Their focus is on each other. But, as time goes on, the honey dries a little and the moon begins to lose its luster. The newness in their relationship begins to wear off, giving way to a different dimension in their relationship.

They begin to know each other on a more intimate level. They can feel each other's hurts and desires. They avoid what will hurt or jeopardize their closeness. They don't hide anything; rather, they express their feelings in confidence and trust. They trust each other with their weaknesses and shortcomings, confident that they will not be used against them. This is the kind of desire that the Lord wants us to enjoy with Him, a close relationship that leads to intimate worship.

O LORD, You have searched me and known me. You know my sitting down and my rising up; You understand my thought afar off. You comprehend my path and my lying down, and are acquainted with all my ways. For there is not a word on my tongue, but behold, O LORD, You know it altogether. You have hedged me behind and before, and laid Your hand upon me. Such knowledge is too wonderful for me; it is high, I cannot attain it. Where can I go from Your Spirit? Or where can I flee from Your presence? If I ascend into heaven, You are there; if I make my bed in hell, behold, You are there. If I take the wings of the morning, and dwell in the uttermost parts of the sea, even there Your hand shall lead me, and Your right hand shall hold me. If I say, "Surely the darkness shall fall on me," even the night shall be light about me; indeed, the darkness shall not hide from You, but the night shines as the day; the darkness and the light are both alike to You. For You formed my inward parts; You covered me in my mother's womb. I will praise You, for I am fearfully and wonderfully made; marvelous are Your works, and that my soul knows very well. My frame was not hidden from You, when I was made in secret, and skillfully wrought in the lowest parts of the earth. Your eyes saw my substance, being yet unformed. And in Your book they all were written, the days fashioned for me, when as yet there were none of them. How precious also are Your thoughts to me, O God! How great is the sum of them! If I should count them, they would be more in number than the sand; when I awake, I am still with You. Oh, that You would slay the wicked, O God! Depart from me, therefore, you bloodthirsty men. For they speak against You wickedly; Your enemies take Your name in vain. Do I not hate them, O LORD, *who hate You? And do I not loathe those who rise up against You? I hate them with perfect hatred; I count them my enemies. Search me, O God, and know my heart; try me, and know my anxieties; and see if there is any wicked way in me, and lead me in the way everlasting* (Psalm 139).

There are different kinds of gods we may find ourselves bowing to. Some of us worship our children. Some worship money. Some worship sin. Some worship themselves while others worship all types of things: a paycheck, reputation, etc.

Who exchanged the truth of God for the lie, and worshiped and served the creature rather than the Creator, who is blessed forever (Romans 1:25).

Have you ever observed a Christian who recently got saved? He worships God with a deep gratitude for his salvation. The first stage in the romance of a man and woman is often referred to as infatuation. This is also typical of the first stage of our relationship with Christ. The dictionary describes infatuation as "to behave foolishly, to inspire with foolish and unreasoning love or attachment."

However, as we mature in the Lord, this type of attraction takes on a new and higher dimension. Infatuation, like romance, operates more on feelings than reality, on the external than on the internal. It is more fleeting than stable, more inconsistent than constant. But mature love is consistent because it is based on commitment. Commitment (covenant) is what sustains any lasting and stable relationship.

COMMITMENT SUSTAINS LASTING AND STABLE RELATIONSHIPS.

When a man first falls in love with a woman, it might have been her beauty and figure that attracted him. But after the marriage, when he wakes up in the morning to bad breath, hair rollers, or a body that has birthed two or three children, infatuation goes out the window. It is neither infatuation nor romance that keeps him coming home, but the commitment to the vow that he made at the altar that sustains the relationship.

The same commitment must define our relationship with the Lord. We must graduate from the point where we praise and worship God only for what He does for us. We must praise Him for who He is. Our worship must transcend a superficial expression that is dependent on our feelings alone. We must develop a relationship that is consistent even in the midst of trials. The trials should deepen our relationship with the Lord, not weaken it.

> *Do you not know that to whom you present yourselves slaves to obey, you are that one's slaves whom you obey, whether of sin leading to death, or of obedience leading to righteousness?* (Romans 6:16)

Wilderness experiences will mature our relationship with the Lord to the degree that our worship is expressed not only externally by the fruit of our lips in praise, but also our love for Him expressed through our continual obedience. It is the obedience that flows from the heart, freely without coercion.

Stamina Secrets and Solutions

1. To truly praise God, you must learn to go beyond yourself and your human limitations. Is it easy to "let go" and praise God with all your heart? If not, what's holding you back?

_____

_____

_____

_____

2. Have you taken advantage of the power that praise and worship wield to break down strongholds in your life?

_____

_____

_____

_____

3. "Praise is replacing your thoughts and the enemy's thoughts with the thoughts of God." Was this a new concept for you to consider? How does this change the way you will praise?

_____

_____

_____

_____

4. Do you realize that music can change attitudes and emotions within you, and that it has the ability to mold and shape thoughts? Knowing this, will you include more music when you praise the Lord?

_____

_____

_____

_____

5. When you praise God, He will give you strength to stand in the midst of any turmoil. Believe.

_____

_____

_____

CHAPTER 12

A Question of Life or Death

In Matthew chapter 13, Jesus told the parable of a good man who sowed good seed in his field, but during the night his enemy came and sowed tares among the wheat. As the plants grew, it became obvious that wheat-like imitations were cropping up along with the wheat. The sower's servants asked the householder, "Didn't you sow good seed in the field? But now we see all of this corruption. Where did these weeds come from?"

> *The kingdom of heaven is like a man who sowed good seed in his field; but while men slept, his enemy came and sowed tares among the wheat and went his way. But when the grain had sprouted and produced a crop, then the tares also appeared. So the servants of the owner came and said to him, "Sir, did you not sow good seed in your field? How then does it have tares?"* (Matthew 13:24-27)

In interpreting this parable, Jesus told His disciples, *"He who sows the good seed is the Son of Man"* (Matt. 13:37).When Jesus, by His Holy Spirit, sows a seed, it's a good seed.

What is "the seed"? The Word of God is the seed that when planted in the fertile ground of a person's heart brings forth spiritual life. When the spiritual seed of God's Word germinates, it results in conception, and conception carried to full term results in the birth of a child of God.

The apostle James says that God, of His own will, gave spiritual birth to us who are the sons and daughters of God by *"the word of truth, that we should be a kind of firstfruits of His creatures"* (James 1:18 KJV). When we become born again by the Spirit of God, we become new creatures, or new creations: *"old things have passed away"* and *"all things have become new"* (2 Cor. 5:17). We are new creations in Christ Jesus.

Once the seed of God has been planted in your heart, you can be assured that no matter what the enemy attempts to plant in your life thereafter, it will (as long as you are faithful to God) never entirely alter the fruit that springs forth from God's pure seed.

Having been born again, not of corruptible seed but of incorruptible, through the word of God, which lives and abides forever (1 Peter 1:23).

God's Word is pure; and once you are born again, God will guard and protect the pure seed He has planted in your heart. He will watch over His Word *"to perform My word"* (Jer. 1:12).

Being a born-again believer in the Lord Jesus is not the same as being a member of any particular religion. Being a child of God and member of the Body of Christ is not dependent upon joining or being accepted by the denomination of choice.

Jesus put it this way: In order to become a citizen of the Kingdom of God, *"You must be born again!"* (See John 3:7b.)

Getting to the Heart of the Problem

When people join a particular religion, they are often seeking to fill a void, or to change their behavior and general outlook on life. This is usually accomplished by some form of behavior modification, such as abstaining from certain meats, wearing certain clothes, and the exercising and keeping of certain rituals and rules. This—like the keeping of the Law of Moses—is referred to as "legalism."

As Christians, however, we should not be bound by rules and regulations, as the apostle Paul explained to the believers at Colosse:

> *Therefore, if you died with Christ from the basic principles of the world, why, as though living in the world, do you subject yourselves to regulations—"Do not touch, do not taste, do not handle," which all concern things which perish with the using—according to the commandments and doctrines of men?* (Colossians 2:20-22).

Without the Spirit of God abiding in one's heart, keeping such laws and rituals is actually impossible. God's Word says in James 2:10 that, *"whoever shall keep the whole law, and yet stumble in one point, he is guilty of all."* If you break one law, you are guilty of breaking all the laws.

Attempting to keep laws and rituals only changes the outward man, not the eternal, hidden man of the heart. And our heart is where the problem begins.

> *The heart is deceitful above all things, and desperately wicked...* (Jeremiah 17:9).

Wickedness is bred into the very fiber of man's soul, as Psalm 51:5 makes clear:

> *Behold, I was brought forth in iniquity, and in sin my mother conceived me.*

The apostle Paul explained to the Roman believers that by the sin of the first man, Adam, all have sinned and entered into death:

Therefore, just as through one man sin entered the world, and death through sin, and thus death spread to all men, because all sinned (Romans 5:12).

As a result:

There is none righteous, no, not one…for all have sinned and fall short of the glory of God (Romans 3:10,23).

In order to be righteous, man needs more than a temporary change in his external behavior. Man needs a change of heart—a new heart:

Then I will give them one heart, and I will put a new spirit within them, and take the stony heart out of their flesh, and give them a heart of flesh, that they may walk in My statutes and keep My judgments and do them; and they shall be My people, and I will be their God (Ezekiel 11:19-20).

Such transformation can only take place supernaturally by the impartation of the Word of God. That is why King David declared, *"Thy word have I hid in mine heart, that I might not sin against thee"* (Ps. 119:11 KJV). When the seed of the Word, the life of God, abides in the believer,

Whoever has been born of God does not sin, for His seed remains in him; and he cannot sin, because he has been born of God (1 John 3:9).

This doesn't mean if you are born again, you will never sin in the flesh. It does mean if you are truly born of the incorruptible seed of the Word of God, you no longer remain a slave to sin. In the life of the born-again, Spirit-filled believer, sin no longer has dominion—not even over the mortal body. Sin doesn't control you; instead, you, by the power of God's Spirit, control sin.

Death Before Life

Today, we seldom hear biblical teaching that emphasizes the death of the flesh by way of the cross. As a result, the Church is in danger of becoming like those whom the apostle Paul called enemies of the cross of Christ (see Phil. 3:18).

Jesus, however, repeatedly stressed the importance of dying to self. He said:

Most assuredly, I say to you, unless a grain of wheat falls into the ground and dies, it remains alone; but if it dies, it produces much grain (John 12:24).

When a seed is planted in the soil, the life germinating within it cannot spring forth until the outer shell of the seed dies off. There, within the dark, damp earth, new life pushes out of its shell, up through the soil, and into the sunlight, where it grows into a plant and begins to produce fruit.

The Word of God declares that seeds produce after their own kind. Whatever is sown in the ground is what comes up. If a corn seed is planted, it will come up as corn on the cob. Likewise, if an apple seed is sown, it will grow into an apple tree.

>+———————————————————+

JESUS CHRIST WAS BURIED IN THE GROUND FOR THE SALVATION OF OUR SOULS.

>+———————————————————+

Accordingly, Jesus Christ, our seed of righteousness, was buried in the ground three days for the salvation of our souls.

Or do you not know that as many of us as were baptized into Christ Jesus were baptized into His death? Therefore we were buried with Him through baptism into death, that just as Christ was raised from the dead by the glory of the

Father, even so we also should walk in newness of life. For if we have been united together in the likeness of His death, certainly we also shall be in the likeness of His resurrection (Romans 6:3-5).

Christ arose on the third day with all power over sin and death, becoming the Seed of eternal life for all who are willing to believe and call on His name. Everyone who believes, rises up with Him to live in newness of life—now and forever.

I am a product of God. Jesus Christ died that I might have life. By the impartation of the Word of God, the Spirit of Christ was made manifest in my spirit. Through the Holy Spirit my soul is sanctified, thereby making me not just a servant, but a legitimate son of God and an heir of salvation.

The Key to Victorious Living

Scripture is very clear on this issue of "flesh death" and "spirit resurrection." There can be no life without death.

The apostle Paul knew this death to the flesh was so crucial to a victorious Christian life that it became the cry of his heart:

That I may know him, and the power of His resurrection, and the fellowship of His sufferings, being conformed to His death (Philippians 3:10).

Some Christians like to quote only the first part of this verse, *"That I may know him, and the power of His resurrection,"* conveniently omitting the remaining portion. They recoil at the thought of knowing Christ in *"the fellowship of His sufferings, being conformed to His death."*

You cannot partake of the power of Christ's resurrection unless you are first willing to lay down your own will and desires and die to all your pride and independence.

Jesus clearly stated:

He who loves his life will lose it, and he who hates his life in this world will keep it for eternal life. If anyone serves Me, let him follow Me; and where I am, there My servant will be also. If anyone serves Me, him My Father will honor (John 12:25-26).

Unless the believer is willing to lose his life for Christ's sake, he can never attain everlasting life. If the Master must suffer to the point of death, so likewise must the servant.

If you're going to live a victorious life, as well as experience and enjoy the power of God in your life, you must do as Jesus commanded and deny yourself, take up your cross daily, and follow Him.

Then He said to them all, "If anyone desires to come after Me, let him deny himself, and take up his cross daily, and follow Me. For whoever desires to save his life will lose it, but whoever loses his life for My sake will save it. For what profit is it to a man if he gains the whole world, and is himself destroyed or lost? (Luke 9:23-25)

When people read Christian books and listen to sermons and teachings, they are usually seeking some type of remedy or solution to a particular pressing issue in life.

If you are searching for the secret of true joy, and victorious Holy Spirit-filled Christ living, the answer is simply this: Die! Die and keep on dying daily until all of you is dead and only Christ lives. Death is the key to life and life more abundantly.

Leave It Alone!

When the servants asked the owner what to do about the strange tares coming up in the field, he said, "Leave them alone until the time of harvest."

So the servants of the owner came and said to him, "Sir, did you not sow good seed in your field? How then does it have tares?" He said to them, "An enemy has done this." The servants said to him, "Do you want us then to go and gather them up?" But he said, "No, lest while you gather up the tares you also uproot the wheat with them. Let both grow together until the harvest, and at the time of harvest I will say to the reapers, 'First gather together the tares and bind them in bundles to burn them, but gather the wheat into my barn'" (Matthew 13:27-30).

Has something unusual and unpleasant sprung up in your life like an unwanted weed? Has it captured and diverted your attention from God's agenda?

God says, "Leave it alone!" He does not want you to be preoccupied or consumed with this distraction at the present time. "Wait until the time of harvest," He says.

God realizes that satanism is having a revival. He knows that the dispersion of illegal drugs and the violence of nations' streets are at an all-time high. The worldwide spread of new incurable diseases like AIDS has not caught Him off-guard.

BELIEVE THAT GOD IS ULTIMATELY IN CONTROL.

Unpleasant situations or undesirable personal issues that you did not expect and did not have any hand in causing may have developed in your life. Such puzzling and unpredictable problems have the potential to distract and move you away from what God is demanding of you right now.

When faced with such situations, we must "cast our cares upon the Lord" (see 1 Peter 5:7). This doesn't mean we should be lazy and irresponsible concerning the affairs of this world. No. We must truly make Jesus Lord of our lives and believe that God is ultimately in control.

Certain challenges and issues will not be fully resolved or overcome until the fulfillment of their purpose has occurred in our lives. We are admonished in Scripture to *"let patience have her perfect work, that ye may be perfect and entire, wanting nothing"* (James 1:4 KJV).

Simply put, there are things in our lives that are not going to be changed until the time of our personal harvest.

The wise preacher, Solomon, said in the writings of Ecclesiastes:

To every thing there is a season, and a time to every purpose under the heaven: a time to be born, and a time to die; a time to plant, and a time to pluck up that which is planted (Ecclesiastes 3:1-2 KJV).

Job said, *"All the days of my hard service I will wait, till my change comes"* (Job 14:14).

There are certain permanent changes that will not be fully executed in our lives until the time of harvest. When that time comes, God will conclude and fulfill every void and set right the wrongs we had to endure during our spiritual winter season. You may have wondered: Why doesn't God set things right sooner?

First of all, God has a divinely ordained purpose for the problems that evolve in our lives. For every affliction and persecution in the life of the Christian believer, there is a God-prescribed purpose. The hand that molds us to become a person who will manifest the character and fruit of the Spirit is the hand of affliction—the right hand of trial and the left hand of tribulation.

The Canvas of Confusion

God shows the excellence of His power against the canvas of confusion. In other words, if all of the conditions necessary for being blessed were comfortable and pleasurable, we would praise the conditions and not praise God, the source of the blessing.

When all of the conditions are adverse and it seems there is no way for us to be blessed, and yet we are blessed anyway, what do we do? We praise God who goes beyond conditions and blesses us in spite of circumstances and in spite of our unworthiness to deserve being blessed.

GOD GOES BEYOND CONDITIONS AND BLESSES US IN SPITE OF OUR UNWORTHINESS.

Until the time of harvest, we must endure certain situations and bondages in our lives that have to be continually overcome. If we encounter situations that seem to get the best of us, we must not become despondent. Even in the midst of trials and tribulations, we can still overcome by the blood of the Lamb and the word of our testimony.

The Bible says when we have *"done all, to stand"* (Eph. 6:13). David prayed, *"Thy word have I hid in mine heart, that I might not sin against Thee"* (Ps. 119:11 KJV).

If we have been diligent to hide the Word of God in our hearts, and if we continue to labor over that Word, we can be assured that in the time of harvest we will reap a bountiful reward—if we faint not.

> *And let us not grow weary while doing good, for in due season we shall reap if we do not lose heart* (Galatians 6:9).

God has predestined a particular and predetermined time that He is going to fulfill all the unfulfilled prophecies, tighten up all the loose ends of life, and make the valleys flat and the crooked places straight.

Eventually, all the seemingly terrible events of your life will fit into the scheme of God's divine omniscient plan. When He unveils the completed picture, it will appear, not as a canvas of confusion, but as a perfect portrait of His love for you.

Stamina Secrets and Solutions

1. "When the spiritual seed of God's Word germinates, it results in conception, and conception carried to full term results in the birth of a child of God." Has the spiritual seed of God's Word been germinated? Carried to full term?

_____

_____

_____

_____

2. "Death is the key to life and life more abundantly." Consider in personal terms what this statement actually means to you—right now, at this point in your life.

_____

_____

_____

_____

3. Is there a circumstance or person in your life that has captured and diverted your attention away from God's agenda? What can you do today to "leave it alone"?

_____

_____

_____

_____

4. Even in the midst of trials and tribulations, you can still
   overcome by the blood of the Lamb and the word of your
   testimony. How often do you claim the blood of the Lamb
   and share your testimony? Is that often enough to overcome your troubles?

   _____

   _____

   _____

   _____

5. "Eventually, all the seemingly terrible events of your life
   will fit into the scheme of God's divine omniscient plan."

   _____

   _____

   _____

CHAPTER 13

Purpose—the Method to the Madness

*And we know that all things work together for good
to them that love God, to them who are the called
according to His purpose* (Romans 8:28 KJV).

When we look at the course of our lives, it sometimes appears to be a chaotic path. The course seems to have no certain direction. Yes, even Christians often find themselves questioning the meaning and course of their lives. The things that God does in our lives, and the incidents and situations that happen, in many instances, appear to be a haphazard, erratic display of a madman who gets pleasure from seeing his subjects suffer and live in despair.

But with God, this is not the case. There is a reason to the riddle. There is an answer to the question, clarity to the confusion, and calmness in the chaos. A bright new day dawns after the dark night. There is a time and a purpose to everything under the sun, a method to the madness.

Knowing God's divine purpose for your life is one of the greatest assets and enablements to help understand and make sense of the perplexities and complications that seem to overwhelm you.

People who possess such knowledge possess power. Jesus displayed an assurance of knowing His purpose in His life and ministry. When people sought to kill Him for His stand and boldness in declaring the truth, He didn't get fearful and back down from what He had said. No! Jesus stood His ground. Why? He knew His purpose. His purpose was to destroy the works of the devil, not be destroyed by the works of the devil.

> *...the devil has sinned from the beginning. For this purpose the Son of God was manifested, that He might destroy the works of the devil* (1 John 3:8).

When you are assured of your purpose, you're not fearful of men or external personal conflicts that attempt to hinder you. Why? Because you know with confidence that sooner or later every trial, every hindering situation, and every opposing person and thing in your life will eventually and inevitably bow and submit to God's plan and purpose for your life. It's just a matter of time and circumstance.

The person who knows his purpose and God-given vision behaves in a strategic, precise, and decisive manner for spiritual warfare. Paul told Timothy to wage a good warfare by the prophecies that went before him. When you know your purpose, you won't sit and passively allow things to occur in your life that are contrary to God's purpose and vision for your life. Neither will you be so quick to get discouraged when situations bring conflict and disorder to your life. You know all things are working together for your good, because you love the Lord and are called according to His purpose. You don't become frustrated or overwhelmed by those things you can't pray away, rebuke away, cast away, fast away, confess away, or speak away. Why? Because you know that if it's in your life, God has allowed it and He wants to use it (since it's there) to transform you into the express image of Christ. He will bring you into that purpose for which you were created. *All* things, not some, work together for the good of those who love the Lord.

Therefore, if you are confused, ready to give up, wondering what's going on and what all the turmoil and chaos you're experiencing is about, ask God, *why?* He just might say, "It's purpose." Maybe He's building a foundation of character in your life. Perhaps it will enable you to obtain the success and blessing that is to be poured into your life. Maybe it is a prelude to the anointing that is about to come upon you. He's got to teach you how to trust Him now, while you are in the desert, so that when you get into the Promised Land and people start acting funny toward you because they're jealous of the anointing on your life, you won't be afraid to cut the ungodly tie.

You know your help comes not from man, but from the Lord. Do you understand what I'm saying? I know you do. If you don't, you'd better ask somebody! But don't just ask anybody, ask the Lord! Call on the Lord and He will answer you. Go ahead. Don't be afraid. Ask Him, "Lord, why?"

CALL ON THE LORD AND HE WILL ANSWER YOU.

Why is there so much strain, why so much struggle, so much conflict, why so much hell? Could it be because I am a man or woman of destiny? Could it be because there's a purpose, a reason for my life? Am I going through so much because I was not brought into this earth haphazardly, but there is actually some divine, ordained logic to my being? Is it true that I'm not some mistake my mother and father made one night in the heat of passion or uncontrollable lust? (If you were born out of wedlock or even as a result of rape, you're not an illegitimate child. What your parents did was illegitimate, not you. You need to know that.)

"God, is it possible that You have a divine motive, a divine reason for my conception? Am I destined, purposed, called to do something great in life? Is it something that nobody else has done, something that nobody else can do but me? My brother can't do it, my sister can't do it, my husband can't do it, my wife can't do it, my pastor can't do it. Is it something so unique to my personality, so common to my life experiences, so relative to my sphere of influence, so dependent upon my color and culture, so necessary to my needs and failures and shortcomings that nobody, no one, can do it exactly the way You want it done but me?"

God's response is, "You're absolutely right!" Just remember, "to whom much is given, much is required" (see Luke 12:48). So get ready for the fire!

Declaring the End From the Beginning

Remember this—fix it in your mind and take it to heart:

*Remember the former things, those of long ago; I am God and there is no other; I am God and there is none like me. I make known **the end from the beginning,** from ancient times, what is still to come. I say: **My purpose will stand, and I will do all that I please** (Isaiah 46:9-10 NIV).*

Wait a minute, God said He is declaring the end from the beginning. That's backward. That's out of sequence. That's out of order. You never declare the end from the beginning. Anybody who tells a good joke will tell you not to tell the punch line before the introduction. God says, "I'll do it backward for you. I declare the end from the beginning. I don't start at the foundation. I reverse the order. I start with the end of it, then I go back and start working on the beginning and make the beginning work into the end." God says, "I establish purpose and then I build procedure."

God says, "I put the victory in the heavenlies, then I start from the earth and move upward. I make sure everything is set according to My design, then I work it out according to My purpose and My plan, My will and My way." That's why God is not nervous when you are nervous, because He has set your end from the beginning. While you're struggling, groping and growling, trying to get it together, and wondering whether you will make it, God knows you're going make it, because He has already set your end!

GOD HAS SET YOUR END FROM THE BEGINNING.

A friend of mine once told me how movies are made. I thought the directors shot the movie scenes in numerical sequence, beginning with the first scene and ending with the last. That is not how it is done. Most times they will shoot the final scene of the movie first. They shoot the last scene first, then roll back the film and start shooting from the beginning, making the beginning work its way into the ending.

Built for a Habitation for God

Now therefore ye are no more strangers and foreigners, but fellow citizens with the saints, and of the household of God; and are built upon the foundation of the apostles and the prophets, Jesus Christ Himself being the chief corner stone; in whom all the building fitly framed together groweth unto an holy temple in the Lord: in whom ye also are builded together for an habitation of God through the Spirit (Ephesians 2:19-22 KJV).

God's approach to destiny is first establishing the purpose, then reverting to the beginning to develop you and instruct you on how to fulfill the purpose. God works out purpose the way you would design and construct a house. If you wanted to build a massive house, you must first hire an architect. The architect takes the vision you have for the house and transforms it on paper (blueprint), establishing what it shall be before it is ever built. Then the carpenter comes in and makes the vision a reality by constructing in material form (manifesting in the present) the design (vision) that the architect has established on paper (the blueprint). Whenever the builder is confused, he refers back to the blueprint. By looking at the blueprint, he knows whether to order steel beams or wood beams, carpet or tile, brick or stucco. Whenever he is unclear about any detail or specification, all he needs to do is check the specifications and look back at what the architect has declared in the design.

I want you to know that God is the Master Architect (designer) and Master Builder all in one. He never gets confused about what is planned or how it is to be built. When God builds something, He builds it for maximum efficiency and optimal performance. We get confused and doubt the outcome. Discouraged, we often find ourselves asking God, "Why did You make me wait while other people go forth? Why does it take so long for my breakthrough to come?" God responds, "What does the blueprint say? What do the specifications call for?"

Many times we wonder why we go through so much persecution. Why do we experience so much rejection that we often feel alienated by those around us just because we love God and want to do His will? God says, "I'm building a solid foundation so you'll be able to *stand under pressure* and be able to go through the storms of life without being moved or shaken." God's response is simple. Anything that is made well is made slowly. "The quality must go in before the name goes on." Anything that is worth having is worth fighting for and worth working hard for.

ANYTHING WORTH HAVING
IS WORTH FIGHTING FOR AND
WORKING HARD FOR.

We also have to know that God is not just building any kind of house. God is building a house of glory, a house filled with His Spirit, governed by His Word (will), and submitted to the lordship of His Son, Jesus Christ. As tenants of that house, we are called to represent the Builder and Lord of that house by manifesting His glory on the earth. God says, "When I get through with you, when I get through nailing on you, when I get through hooking your two-by-fours together and putting windows in, when I get through hanging siding on you and placing bricks on your frame, then you are going to be a glorious edifice, a sight for the world to see." Still the house is not for us to be glorified, but that God might be exalted and glorified.

But we have this treasure in earthen vessels, that the excellence of the power may be of God and not of us (2 Corinthians 4:7).

Vision (Revelation) and Purpose

Where there is no revelation [vision], *the people cast off restraint [perish]; but happy is he who keeps the law* [Word of God] (Proverbs 29:18).

Solomon declared in the Book of Proverbs that where there is no vision (no divine and fresh revelation from God), the people perish (they lose control and cast off restraint).

If you are a person without direction, purpose, meaning, or understanding of God's specific intent for your life, it could very well mean that you lack vision. You may lack a personal revelation, which is God's divine insight into the reason for your being and the reason for your living. Vision not only gives meaning and understanding of one's purpose in life, it also gives one wisdom on how to bring it to pass. Vision gives understanding and reveals meaning to the trials you may experience at any given time.

VISION GIVES UNDERSTANDING AND REVEALS MEANING TO THE TRIALS.

God imparts to you a revelation of His plans for your life. That is how vision begins. Then in some cases, God confirms that word He spoke personally to you through a prophecy given to you by another man or woman of God. If you try to figure out the fulfillment of the prophecy by looking at your present situation, circumstance, or condition, it may be hard to believe without the assurance of faith and the witness of the Holy Spirit. Why would it be so hard to believe? Because when God gives you a vision, it is always too great and complex for you in your own power and ability to bring about; it is *"Not by might, nor by power, but by My spirit saith the LORD..."* (Zech. 4:6 KJV).

God calls those things that are not as though they were. He calls you in the present what you're going to be in the future, and then makes you prove His Word to be true. Hence the Scripture says, *"Let God be true, but every man a liar"* (Rom. 3:4). It means you embrace what God has said about you over what everybody else has said about you, good or bad. When all has been said and done, God proves what He has said about you. It comes through His written Word and His personal revelation to you. His Word is right and everyone who speaks contrary to that Word is a liar.

Your life will witness the validity of God's Word if you continue to walk by faith and obey the Father. You will prove to this world that God is real and that He's able. There is nothing else in life that pleases God the Father more.

*If that is the case, our **God whom we serve is able** to deliver us from the burning fiery furnace, and He will deliver us from your hand, O king* (Daniel 3:17).

*…Indeed, he will be made to stand, for **God is able** to make him stand* (Romans 14:4).

*Put on the whole armor of **God**, that you may be **able to stand** against the wiles of the devil* (Ephesians 6:11).

Jesus proved the validity of God's Word when He rose from the dead. This was true regardless of the Romans, Jews, skeptics, and doomsayers who did not believe in His divinity.

My brothers and sisters, you must continue to obey and serve God. You are going to show your critics and the unbelievers that you, as the servant of God, will win in the end. Some critics will bet against you and they will speak against you. They will say, "That girl ain't never gonna be nothing. Her mama was nothing. Her aunt was nothing. I knew her grandmother and she was nothing. Her granddaddy was nothing. Her father was nothing and she is going to be nothing." According to the Word of God:

If anyone is in Christ, he is a new creation; old things have passed away; behold, all things have become new (2 Corinthians 5:17).

God said that we are going to make a liar out of all of them. He says, "I will remain true and every man a liar."

You may have been lying to yourself, telling yourself you aren't anything. You are telling yourself you're no good, but you ought to believe God. Believe Him in spite of your feelings or emotions. Stop believing those lying prophecies of the past: relatives and friends who claimed you would never amount to anything. Stop believing people and teachers who called you stupid. Turn a deaf ear to racism which said because you're black you are not important, sexists who said because you're a woman you're not important. Stop believing the lies of men. Become renewed to the truth of God. You might have had a bad childhood and have been abused, misused, rejected, and neglected. God says forget those things that are behind you and reach forth to those things that are before you. Press toward the mark of your high calling in Christ Jesus (see Phil. 3:13-14).

> *He is our father in the sight of God in whom he believed— the God who gives life to the dead and calls things that are not as though they were* (Romans 4:17b NIV).

> *No longer will you be called Abram, your name will be Abraham, for I have made you a father of many nations* (Genesis 17:5 NIV).

"Calling those things that be not as though they were." The emphasis in this particular context (Rom. 4:18) is not on Abraham or any believer calling things that be not as though they were, but on *God* calling those things that be not as though they were. It is God, through His Word, speaking into existence His will, not man's will. We should be very glad that it is God and not man. I wouldn't want a man to have the power to determine my future and destiny.

It is God who calls those things that be not as though they were. Our responsibility is to line our will up with His will. When we do, our lives become empowered by the grace and Spirit of God to accomplish what normally would be humanly impossible. That is the essence of authentic prophecy that comes from the heart of God.

THE JUST SHALL LIVE BY FAITH.

If we continue to walk by faith, believing in the prophetic word that God has spoken over our lives, things that may seem impossible to realize in the natural shall come to pass.

The just shall live by faith, and anything that is not of faith is sin (see Rom. 1:17; 14:23). For we walk by faith and not by sight (the physical senses, i.e. emotions, mental reasoning, or the things that we can visibly see). When God speaks a word into our lives, as far as He is concerned, it has already been accomplished. If the purpose has already been completed, the task or assignment has already been done, it is in essence a finished work. He calls those "things which be not as though they were" (Rom. 4:17b KJV).

Hebrews 10:14 KJV declares that God offered Christ as the ultimate sacrifice for man's sin and has *"perfected forever them that are sanctified."* The word *perfected* in this particular passage of Scripture means in the Greek to bring to an end by completing or perfecting the accomplishment of bringing to completeness. This simply means that the end is already finished. It came by the supernatural power and grace given to us by what Christ accomplished during His crucifixion and resurrection.

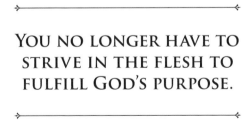

YOU NO LONGER HAVE TO STRIVE IN THE FLESH TO FULFILL GOD'S PURPOSE.

Therefore we no longer have to strive in the flesh in order to fulfill God's purpose. The calling for our lives has already been determined in Heaven. It is a complete and finished work. Your purpose in the sight of God is already an accomplished thing, waiting for your fulfillment.

Perfected means completely over, settled, done, and concluded. God says, "I have perfected your life and purpose for life. I fix them, I set their course in stone. You don't have to run and see what the end is going to be." God said that it's already accomplished. The thing you're worried about performing, God said it is already done.

What about all the debris in your life? What about all of those loose ends and uncertain things that Charles Dickens talked about in his book, *A Tale of Two Cities?* He said, "Life is a tale told by a fool," but God tells a different story. He says:

> *And we know that all things work together for good to those who love God, to those who are the called according to His purpose* (Romans 8:28).

In order to walk with God, you've got to be willing to hear some things that sound foolish. Often times, obeying God does seem like "a tale told by a fool."

Come on Up Here

God called Moses upon Mount Sinai and said, "Come on up here. I'm going to show you My purpose, what My plan shall be." Moses walked upon the mountain saying, "Yes, Lord, what's going on?" The Lord said, "This is what is about to take place. There's a boy down there in your church (camp) named Aaron. Aaron is to be appointed as a high priest. I'm making him an outfit: a garment symbolizing My pattern of holiness, righteousness, and My set and divine way of communicating to My people. The outfit will have a breastplate with twelve stones, each one representing one of the twelve tribes of Israel—My chosen people. I'm getting him together, girding his loins about with truth. When I get through with him, he shall be a glorious and beautiful sight for eyes to see.

Aaron shall be the one who will be able to go in and out before Me." Anybody can attempt to come in before God, but it takes a holy person to come out living. God told Moses when nobody else can be in His presence and live, Aaron will be anointed to come in and go out alive.

Aaron sounds like a pretty good fellow, but while God was declaring to Moses about Aaron's perfected state, He was already taking care of Aaron's end, calling those things that are not as though they were. Aaron was down at the bottom of the mountain, working on the beginning. If you were to judge from Aaron's beginning, you would not believe what was promised to this guy. As a matter of fact, the guy was down the mountain engrossed in idol worship, worshiping a golden calf. The guy just didn't have it going on. He was an idolater. He was the head of the hypocrites, president of the failures, chairman of the defeated, busy building a golden calf unto a strange god.

When Moses came down the mountain, he began to build up Aaron, exhorting him on who he was and what God called him to do and be. Moses got the revelation of the end. Moses says, "Hey man, (I'm paraphrasing), oohhh God has designed an outfit for you…. Blood, you're going to be laid out, you are going to be too sharp."

I know what you probably would have said. Something like, "Lord God, do You know where he is? Do You know what he's doing?" You don't believe God knew what he was doing?

Remember, God sets the end from the beginning, calling those things that are not as though they were. God declares even to you today, as you read this book, that, "In spite of what you've done, in spite of how you've failed, in spite of how you've messed up, in spite of how you have suffered, in spite of how many times you have given up and almost died, I want you to know that My grace is sufficient for you. My grace will enable you to be victorious and make it through to complete your journey (purpose). I've shed blood for you and given sacrifices for you. When I get through washing, molding, and making you into what I've already declared you are, you will show the world how glorious I am."

That No Flesh Shall Glory in His Sight

Brothers, think of what you were when you were called. Not many of you were wise by human standards; not many were influential; not many were of noble birth. But God chose the foolish things of the world to shame the wise; God chose the weak things of the world to shame the strong. He chose the lowly things of this world and the despised things and the things that are not—to nullify the things that are…. That no flesh should glory in His presence (1 Corinthians 1:26-28 NIV; 1:29 KJV).

God doesn't seek to manifest His glory and glorious works through those whom the world perceives as great and wonderful. He boldly declares without apology or apprehension that, "My ways are not your ways, My thoughts are higher than your thoughts" (see Isa. 55:8). When people seek individuals to do great and monumental things, they look for those who have great education, wealth, prestige, and honor; a man of great nobility. But God selects those who are like bums. He chooses those whom the world has rejected; those who have been ostracized and alienated from family, friends, and peers; those who are constantly criticized. God takes them and makes them and infuses them with His power, revelation, and wisdom so that they can be wondrously educated in the things of God. This occurs so that they can greatly change and affect the things of the world.

GOD INFUSES YOU WITH HIS POWER, REVELATION, AND WISDOM.

God considers those of no account, those nobody expects to be anything; those whose family, friends, and relatives have thrown away and given up on. God takes those who are fearful and don't believe in themselves and makes them men and women of greatness with wealth, prestige, and honor—mighty men and women of valor! These are men and women like Abraham, Joseph, Gideon, Jacob, Peter, Deborah, Ruth, Esther, Mary, William J. Seymour, Oral Roberts, Bishop Mason of the Church of God in Christ, Aimee Semple McPherson of the Foursquare Church, and Kathryn Kuhlman, just to name a few. Why does God do this? Why does God use the rejected and the despised?

It's a simple but profound answer: that He, God, would get all the glory and not man, *"that no flesh should glory in his presence."* For the Word of God says that, *"we have this treasure in earthen vessels, that the excellence of the power may be of God, and not of us"* (2 Cor. 4:7). It is God and not you.

God says, "When I bring you out, your critics will know it was Me. I'm going to wait until you fail; I'm going to wait until you lose confidence in yourself, your education, your job, your influential title, your résumés, your friends, your family, your doctrines, your creed, and your denominational affiliation. When you've lost hope in everything earthly and feel totally worthless and are in complete despair, then I'm going to stretch forth My right hand. I'm going to pick up your feet out of the miry clay. I'm going to place you on a rock to stay. When nobody else will praise Me, praise will continually be in your mouth, because you are going to know it was My right hand and My holy arm that brought you victory. It was I who brought you out. It was I who gave you a breakthrough, and not yourself or the help of man."

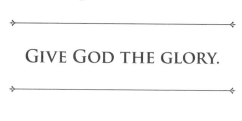

GIVE GOD THE GLORY.

Do you still wonder why you have had to go through all the pain and hell you have been experiencing since getting serious with God and vowing to obey Him, no matter what the cost? The reason is that you would no longer place confidence in the flesh, for it is God who works in you both to will and to do His good will and pleasure (see Phil. 2:13). But in all things we must give Him the praise, not man, *"that no flesh should glory in His presence"* (1 Cor. 1:29).

Stamina Secrets and Solutions

1. "Knowing God's divine purpose for your life is one of the greatest assets and enablements to help understand and make sense of the perplexities and complications that seem to overwhelm you." Do you know your divine purpose?

_____

_____

_____

_____

2. "God's approach to destiny is first establishing the purpose, then reverting to the beginning to develop you and instruct you on how to fulfill the purpose." Trusting God and listening for His direction brings you into your purpose.

_____

_____

_____

_____

3. To walk with God, you've got to be willing to hear some things that sound foolish. Are you willing?

_____

_____

_____

_____

4. God doesn't seek to manifest His glory and glorious works through those whom the world perceives as great and wonderful. Do you believe He can use you to manifest His glory and works?

_____

_____

_____

5. Do you still wonder why you have had to go through all the pain and hell you have been experiencing since getting serious with God and vowing to obey Him, no matter what the cost?

_____

_____

_____

CHAPTER 14

Water in the Wilderness

For thus says the LORD, "You shall not see wind,
*nor shall you see rain; **yet that valley shall be***
***filled with water...**" (2 Kings 3:17).*

Can you still believe this promise after all you have been
through—after suffering and being deprived of winds and
rain? God said He is going to give you the water. Since the king of
Moab did not see rain, he apparently did not expect to see water.
And when he came upon the mountain top, and looked down in
the valley, the rays of the sun on the water gave the appearance of
blood. He thought it was the blood of his enemies. He ran down
there to kill them, but what he thought was blood was water.

Maybe you should have been dead and long gone, but God
saw your blood and sent you the water. You could have died of
spiritual dehydration, but He did not send wind or rain, *just water.*
You could have given up, but you did *not* give up.

For whatever things were written before were written for our
*learning, that we through the **patience** and comfort of the*
Scriptures might have hope (Romans 15:4).

I could have passed out, but I am not out. There is water in my family, water in my relationships, water in my church, water in my preaching, water in my business, water in my home, water in my career, water, water, water, water…water everywhere.

There are some people in the wilderness who don't have any water yet, and unless they have someone to minister to them as Elisha ministered to Jehoshaphat and Jehoram, they will die in the wilderness without water. Someone must preach the gospel until their dry areas are made wet.

> …*that you may enter the land which the LORD your God is giving you, "a land **flowing** with milk and honey," just as the LORD God of your fathers promised you* (Deuteronomy 27:3).

You don't have to give up, you don't have to give in, you don't have to quit. God said He will fill those dry areas of your life with water.

DON'T GIVE UP. DON'T GIVE IN. DON'T QUIT.

If you have been going though dry places and wilderness for a long time, God is saying, "Dig some ditches, because I'm getting ready to bless you and your latter day is going to be greater than your former day." God will fill the ditches in your home and marriage with water. To the ditches of finances, God says, "I will fill them with water."

To the ditches of your emotions, He says, "Get your mind ready, get your attitude right, get your heart fixed, because when I open up the windows of Heaven I am going to pour you out a blessing that you will not have room enough to receive" (see Mal. 3:10).

> *Give, and it will be given to you: good measure, pressed down, shaken together, and running over will be put into*

your bosom. For with the same measure that you use, it will be measured back to you (Luke 6:38).

It is a blessing that will be pressed down, shaken together, and running over. Are you ready for the blessing? Some people may be thinking of quitting, but don't quit. The moment that you are ready to throw in the towel, when you think you cannot take it any more, it is then that God will send you His blessing. Do not allow satan to discourage you and thus deprive you of God's blessing. The devil is a liar and the father of lies.

You are of your father the devil, and the desires of your father you want to do. He was a murderer from the beginning, and does not stand in the truth, because there is no truth in him. When he speaks a lie, he speaks from his own resources, for he is a liar and the father of it (John 8:44).

God repeats, "Dig ditches in your valley. Get ready! You have been suffering for a long time, but I am getting ready to bless you. I want you to dig ditches and get ready. As soon as you are ready, the answer will be there." When the answer comes, it is going to come in the spirit and not in the flesh. Once the ditches have been dug, there will be no warning or sign, no clouds, no winds, not even rain, *just water.*

In the natural when it is about to rain, one can tell by the wind and the clouds, but God is saying, "I'm going to send you a blessing that has no sign, and it will not have any warning. Everything may be stagnant, but I am going to move in the midst of your stagnation. Just because you do not see any wind does not mean that I am not getting ready to bless you. Get ready!"

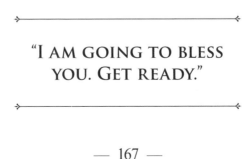

"I AM GOING TO BLESS YOU. GET READY."

You might look up and not see any sign in the climate. Maybe you do not see the clouds forming in the sky. I know you are used to lightning, but there might not be any. I know that you are used to thunder before the outpouring, but you may not hear the thunder. There might not be wind. It might not even rain, but just because there is no wind, nor rain, does not mean that there won't be water.

You must know that God is going to bless you. I don't care if the wind is not blowing or the thunder is not sounding, you must know that God cannot lie. If He has promised to bless you, then He will bless you. If He has promised to deliver you, then He will deliver you. If He has promised to bring you out, then He is able. The Lord is more than able. No wind, no rain, but there will still be blessing without warning. *You must expect the blessing to come.*

When God was ready to send the flood, He did not just send water down on Noah. The Bible says that He broke up the cisterns of the deep, and water started coming up out of the ground (see Gen. 7:11). Yes, water started coming out of the dry places.

Do you have any dry places? God is saying that is where the water is going to come from. Have you had struggles in any areas of your life? God says that is where the water is going to come from. Do you have frustrations? God says He is going to send the water out of your pain and agony.

> *...To give them beauty for ashes, the oil of joy for mourning, the garment of praise for the spirit of heaviness; that they may be called trees of righteousness, the planting of the* LORD, *that He may be glorified* (Isaiah 61:3).

Maybe the water is trickling at first. Have you ever said, "I'm getting something, but that is not enough. I am better than what I used to be, but I still don't have that breakthrough. I am not saying that You are not blessing me, Lord, but something is missing out of my blessings. I am getting a little moisture?" But God is telling you now to wait on Him. You must learn how to wait. It is they that wait upon the Lord whose strength God will renew.

Wait on the LORD; *be of good courage, and* ***He shall strengthen your heart;*** *wait, I say, on the LORD!* (Psalm 27:14)

The Word of God says to wait. Wait even when it seems that nothing is happening. Wait while you are in the midst of the wilderness, when there is no sign of water. Wait on the perfect timing of God. Remember that He has a plan. He has not forsaken you even though the devil might have given you the impression that He has.

> *But those who wait on the* LORD *shall* ***renew their strength;*** *they shall mount up with wings like eagles, they shall run and not be weary, they shall walk and not faint* (Isaiah 40:31).

As you wait, the Lord says, "Mount up with wings like eagles, run and don't be weary, walk and don't faint because that little drip of water is turning into a trickle, and the trickle will turn into a stream, and the stream will turn into a creek, the creek is going to turn into a lake, and the lake is going to turn into a river. And out of you, as the Word says, will flow rivers of living water"

> *"He who believes in Me, as the Scripture has said, out of his heart* ***will flow rivers of living water"*** (John 7:38). God will send you some water that will come out of your wilderness, and when it comes, it will be more than enough.

If you do not have wind, do not worry.
If you do not see rain, do not be perturbed.
God is still going to give you the water. If you want the outpouring of God's Spirit, wait for Him. God will send you water in your dry places. God will send the water right into your personal wilderness.

Water in the Wilderness

> *And all the congregation of the children of Israel journeyed from the wilderness of Sin, after their journeys, according to the commandment of the LORD, and pitched in Rephidim: and there was no water for the people to drink…. And the people thirsted for water; and the people murmured against Moses, and said, Wherefore is this that thou hast brought us up out of Egypt, to kill us and our children and our cattle with thirst?…And the LORD said unto Moses, Go on before the people, and take with thee of the elders of Israel; and thy rod, wherewith thou smotest the river, take in thine hand, and go. Behold, I will stand before thee there upon the rock in Horeb; and thou shall smite the rock, and there shall come water out of it, that the people may drink. And Moses did so in the sight of the elders of Israel* (Exodus 17:1,3,5-6 KJV).

There is water in the wilderness. If you are going through the dry places, is it not wonderful to know that God is a cool drink while in a hot and thirsty land? When you run out of water, run out of friends, run out of ideas, and run out of plans, God says, "You are going through a tough time, but do not worry; I have a plan."

> ***Blessed be the God and Father of our Lord Jesus Christ***, *the Father of mercies and God of all comfort,* ***who comforts us in all our tribulation,*** *that we may be able to comfort those who are in any trouble, with the comfort with which we ourselves are comforted by God. For as the sufferings of Christ abound in us, so our consolation also abounds through Christ* (2 Corinthians 1:3-5).

God has a way of escape. I do not know what wilderness you are going through, but I do know this much about God: He will step into the middle of the wilderness of your dilemma. He is not confined to the church building. He is also God in your wilderness.

He will come into your house. He will come on your job. He will take care of you. Have you ever found yourself praising God in the car, and the praise reaches a height where tears well up in your eyes, and you know you must stop the car for fear that you might hit someone? Have you been in a situation where you are worshiping God, and people around you thought that you were talking to yourself?

Has the Lord ever visited you in an awkward place, such as the bus stop or a subway, where you really do not have the freedom to praise God? However, the praise got so high within you that it took every muscle of your will power to keep quiet.

ENJOY BEING YOURSELF WITH GOD.

I enjoy being by myself with God. If I shout too loud in public, and the people get nervous, I cannot be very free. But when I am alone, I can call on God as loud as I want, and I can cry as long and as loud as I want to cry. If I want to tap my foot, I can tap my foot. If I feel like moaning, I can lie down and moan without the fear that someone is commenting about it. When I wave my hands, He understands.

You may be in a dry place where there is no water. Or you may be in the wilderness or in a deep valley, but remember, God provides water in the dry places.

When I was in Arizona on a preaching tour, I had a chance to see a dry riverbed. As I walked down into the dry riverbed, I sensed in my spirit that the Lord was ministering to me. Once there was water in the riverbed, but now it had gone dry. Yet, you could tell that there used to be water there, but due to the dryness in the atmosphere, it had dried up. It is amazing that the sun was able to evaporate that much water. The rocks could still be seen at the bottom of the riverbed. Yet no life existed there.

Unfortunately, this is the way some churches are today. There once was water in these churches. There used to be some glory in their midst. The church used to be spiritually alive, but now there is no sign of life.

> *O* LORD, *the hope of Israel, all who forsake You shall be ashamed. "Those who depart from Me shall be written in the earth, because they have forsaken* **the LORD, the fountain of living waters**" *(Jeremiah 17:13).*

A principle needs to be underscored here. If the river dried up over here, then you must go over there. If you are going through a dry time in your life, then you must find water. If you do not find some water, you will be like those animals that died without water.

I am conscious of the fact that I need some water every hour of the day. I am not in need of someone who would beat me over the head with the Word just to make me feel bad, but I do need someone who can tell me that I can make it. I need someone to tell me that God is my Deliverer, that He is my Joy in the midst of sorrow, that He is my Healer, the One who makes a way where there seems to be none.

> *And the ransomed of the* LORD *shall return, and come to Zion with singing, with everlasting joy on their heads.* **They shall obtain joy and gladness,** *and sorrow and sighing shall flee away* (Isaiah 35:10).

> *For You have been a shelter for me, a* **strong tower** *from the enemy. I will abide in Your tabernacle forever; I will trust in the shelter of Your wings* (Psalm 61:3-4).

> *The name of the* LORD *is a* **strong tower***; the righteous run to it and are safe* (Proverbs 18:10).

I need someone to tell me He is a strong Tower, that He is the Doctor in the sick room, the Lawyer in the courtroom, and the Water in the wilderness. God says, "This is what I want you to do while you are still down in the dry riverbed: dig ditches in your valley." Now it may have been enough for God to fill your riverbed, but God says He is going to bless you much more than the riverbed can contain.

God says, "You had better begin to dig those ditches in the riverbed, because what you need is not deep enough for My supply, and when I do bless you, My blessing is going to be so much greater than your present capacity to receive. So dig some ditches for the outpouring. Contrary to how bleak and distraught the situation may be or how devastating the trial or crisis, remember My promise: I will provide water in the wilderness."

Stamina Secrets and Solutions

1. Are you ready for the blessing God wants to give you to overflowing? What must you do to be prepared to receive all that He wants to give you?

   _____

   _____

   _____

   _____

2. "The Word of God says to wait. Wait even when it seems that nothing is happening." How patient are you? Does waiting on God seem impossible? The Holy Spirit will give you the strength to stand while waiting on His perfect timing.

   _____

   _____

   _____

   _____

3. If the river of God's Word has dried up in your church, you must find water to survive. Are you being fed the bread and water of life? Consider your diet seriously.

   _____

   _____

   _____

4. God is your Deliverer, your Joy in the midst of sorrow, your Healer, the One who makes a way where there seems to be none. Have you thanked Him today for all He has done and will do for you?

_____

_____

_____

5. God has promised to provide water in every personal wilderness you encounter throughout life. Will you drink of His life-giving waters? Choose now.

_____

_____

_____

CHAPTER 15

Superman Is Dead

The best parts of school when I was an eight-year-old were recess and the walk home from school. I liked recess because it gave me an opportunity to stretch my legs and play with my friends. I liked the walk home from school because I usually had a quarter buried deep within my pocket, hidden somewhere beneath the bubble gum, the baseball cards, and all the other paraphernalia that eight-year-olds think are valuable.

I would save that quarter until we walked down Troy Road toward "old man Harless'" store. Now, that was what we called him if we were sure he wasn't around. But if we saw him, he immediately became "Mr. Harless," complete with "Yes, sir," and "No, sir," and all the other polite things we were instructed to say lest the seats of our pants perish in the fires of my mother's wrath!

That quarter of mine was saved for the brightly colored books that were stacked in a display for all the children to see. There were all of my old friends...Superman and Captain Marvel, Captain America and Spiderman. I would purchase a copy of the latest issue and hurry a little farther down Troy Road. Once I found the old path that led up the hill behind the house, I would start my ascent to the big rock beneath the apple tree. There, hidden from public scrutiny, I would pull out my prized hero magazine and imagine that I was one of these men, a superhero who could transform as needed into anything necessary to destroy the villain.

I know all of this sounds terribly old-fashioned. Maybe it sounds a little too much like a scene that should include Andy Griffith, Aunt Bea, and the whole Mayberry clan, but that was really how it was in the days before children started carrying guns instead of comic books. I grew up reading about heroes. We believed in possibility, and though we were neither wealthy nor affluent, we could escape like a bird through the window of a full-color magazine and become anybody we wanted to be for at least 30 minutes—before my mother's voice would be heard from the rickety back porch behind the house.

Where Did the Heroes Go?

We need heroes today. We need someone to believe in and look up to. We need someone who has accomplished something to give us the courage to believe in the invisible and feel the intangible. We need role models and men whose shadows we may stand in, men who provide a cool refreshing place of safety away from the despair of our oppressive society. It's just that all the "supermen" in the Church seem to have somehow gotten zapped by "kryptonite." Either they or their reputations have wilted into the abyss of human failure.

What are we going to do as we face this generation? From drug-using political officials to prostitute-purchasing preachers, the stars are falling on the heads of this generation! All of their wonder and dreams have turned into a comic book—a comic book that somehow doesn't seem funny anymore. Where did the heroes go?

This isn't just a church issue. We're suffering from an eroding sense of family, not just of family values. The entire concept of the family, period, has been crumbling because of this society's growing acceptance of non-traditional families. More and more women have chosen to be mothers without choosing fathers, while others have become single parents by necessity, not by choice. The gay community has added to the confusion by establishing "homes" that do not reflect God's original plan for child-rearing. So now we have twisted homes that are producing twisted children.

There is a cry coming up out of the city streets: Our fathers went out for coffee and came back with cocaine. Their hands will not tuck us in because their feet are shackled to the prison floor. Mother is out of milk and brother just joined a gang. Even in the neighborhood we used to drive through and dream that we lived in, we see ambulances. Moving vans just moved Mommy away from Daddy, and now we see them by appointment.

The whole country has fallen into the trash can like discarded comic books whose story lines are out-of-date. Where are the heroes?

Honesty Before God

Our healing will require more than a processional of religious ideas that are neither potent nor relevant. We need to understand that God is able to repair the broken places, but it requires us to expose where those broken places are. If we don't say to Him, "This is where I am hurting," then how can He pour in the oil and the wine?

GOD IS ABLE TO REPAIR THE BROKEN
PLACES, BUT WE MUST EXPOSE
WHERE THOSE BROKEN PLACES ARE.

We need to lay ourselves before Him and seek His face in the beauty of holiness—the holiness that produces wholeness. This isn't a matter of one denomination arguing with another over who is right; it is a matter of a broken family seeking healing and answers that can only come from the presence of God. I am convinced He can heal whatever we can confess!

> *Come, and let us return to the LORD; for He has torn, but He will heal us; He has stricken, but He will bind us up* (Hosea 6:1).

It is in these moments that we are forced to reevaluate our concepts. Have we misaligned ourselves with God, or were our goals "out of kilter" to begin with? I really believe that we have made the unfortunate error of Old Testament Israel, whose attempt to attain righteousness produced a self-righteous mentality in many.

HE CAN HEAL WHATEVER WE CAN CONFESS!

The Old Testament expressed the righteousness of God, a righteousness that the New Testament fully revealed in the gospel of Jesus Christ. Although the Old Testament could not completely reveal the righteousness of God, it certainly introduced a concept of how God defines holiness to humanity and Israel.

God knew that the children of Israel would fail in their attempts to achieve the morality contained in the Law. Through their failures, God wanted the Israelites to find the redemption that He had allocated through the blood. Unfortunately, instead of honestly confessing to God the enormity of their failure, they became increasingly hypocritical. The whole purpose of the Law was spoiled because the fleshly egos of men would not repent and seek divine assistance for justification.

For I am not ashamed of the gospel of Christ: for it is the power of God to salvation for everyone who believes, for the Jew first, and also for the Greek. For in it the righteousness of God is revealed from faith to faith; as it is written, "The just shall live by faith" (Romans 1:16-17).

It takes great courage to exemplify total honesty with God. We have not even been totally released to admit our insufficiencies with others, and sometimes even with ourselves. How tragic! When we discover our own limitations, we become eligible to discover the all-sufficiency of God. Here we *stand in strength,* like Israel in tainted armor, before the presence of a God whose brilliancy dims the radiant brightness of the sun. Yet there is a method to the madness of our predicament.

God knew who we were when He called us. Perhaps the sharp contrast between the people God uses and the God who uses them is to provide the worshiper with a clear distinction of who is to be worshiped!

Real Heroes

It is undeniable that we face faltering visions and visionaries. Let us seek God for His divine purpose. Could it possibly be that God's intent is to establish believable heroes?

We need no glaring, gleaming, high-polished people for this day! We need heroes whose tarnished suits cannot hide their open hearts or their need to touch broken lives. The cry is going out for something believable—for something that even if not glorious, is at least fathomable.

The stress of trying to impress others with elitist presentations of spiraling spiritual altitudes has produced isolation and intimidation. No wonder our leaders are dying in the pulpit and suffering from an epidemic of heart attacks and strokes! It is hard to take an ordinary man from an ordinary background, saddle him with responsibility and tremendous visibility, and tell him, "You must be god-like."

Writing in all honesty, the greatest of the apostles—the writer of most of the New Testament epistles—confessed that though he aspired to "apprehend," he hadn't attained (see Phil. 3:12). In what area did this apostle fail? The Holy Spirit has granted him some semblance of diplomatic immunity that at least affords him the right of privacy in spite of imperfections. Yet we continually eat a perfect word from his stained hands, a word that converts the soul and challenges the most godly among us. I speak, of course, of the apostle Paul himself!

> *Brethren, I do not count myself to have apprehended; but one thing I do, forgetting those things which are behind and reaching forward to those things which are ahead, I press toward the goal for the prize of the upward call of God in Christ Jesus* (Philippians 3:13-14).

Alas, the call is a high calling, an upward call. Yet it has been answered by lowly people who had the discernment to see a God high and lifted up. They stood on their toes like children, but still fell short of reaching His splendor. In short, the heroes in the Bible were not perfect, but they were powerful! They were not superhuman, but they were revelatory. Often chastised and corrected, they were still not discarded, for the Lord was with them.

Jesus was forever having to correct His disciples. Their pettiness, their anger and stinginess—these faults often reaffirmed the fact that they were *"men of like passions"* (Acts 14:15 KJV). I, for one, am glad that they were. Their human frailties encourage the rest of us that we too can be used by God in spite of our feeble, crippled, and fragmented attempts at piety and true devotion.

What Makes a Hero?

At the risk of tarnishing a record that no one believes anyway, could we reevaluate what a hero really is? Isn't a hero someone who puts himself at risk to help someone else? Is it someone whose unselfish heart allows him to take dangerous risks to accomplish definite results to help someone else? I wonder if some of the men and women whom we say "failed" actually tarnished their records by having the courage to climb high enough to take the risks that others would not be willing to take...in order to help others.

No, let's not glamorize sin. Sin is sin and it stinks in the nostrils of God. But have our noses become more sensitive than God's? Would we, like the others outside the tomb, choose to condemn to an eternal grave the man Lazarus, whose decomposing body had been shut up in a tomb for three days and begun to stink? Thank God that Jesus didn't let the stink stop Him from saving the man.

⤞————————————————————⤝

SIN IS SIN AND IT STINKS IN THE NOSTRILS OF GOD.

⤞————————————————————⤝

You have to be a hero to even expose yourself to the jealousy and cruelty of being raised up as a leader. Leaders are ostracized by their peers and criticized by their subordinates. They serve valiantly, though they often receive blows from satan and stabs from friends. Through it all, they continue to minister as if all were well.

I pause to lift to the throne every man or woman of God who is under attack by the enemy. Whether it be a financial, spiritual, or moral attack, I pray for you, my silent, alienated, wounded physician. May the medicine you have given to others come to your aid and bless you. May you recover all that satan desires to destroy in your life! In Jesus' name, amen!

These all died in faith, not having received the promises, but having seen them afar off were assured of them, embraced them and confessed that they were strangers and pilgrims on the earth. For those who say such things declare plainly that they seek a homeland (Hebrews 11:13-14).

It is imperative that our vision be both progressive and regressive. In the forefront of our minds must be a plan that promises bright hopes for the future. I often say that a man cannot die with a twinkle in his eye! *There must be a strong sense of destiny lodged firmly in our minds that dispels the despair of past failures.* We must live our lives facing the rising sun.

Although heroes don't have to be perfect, I realize they must be people who are resilient enough to survive tragedy and adversity. All of us have experienced the pain of adversity in our warfare, whether it was a physical, emotional, economical, spiritual, or sexual attack. Regardless of which category the attack falls under, they are very personal in nature. Real heroes not only survive the incident, but also overcome the lingering side effects that often come from it.

REAL HEROES SURVIVE THE INCIDENT AND OVERCOME THE LINGERING SIDE EFFECTS.

Why do I say that? If you don't survive, you can't save anyone. No young man in a combat zone can carry his wounded comrade if he himself does not survive. Live long enough to invest the wealth of your experience in the release of some other victim whom satan desires to bind or incapacitate!

And truly, if they had been mindful of that country from whence they came out, they might have had opportunity to have returned (Hebrews 11:15 KJV).

The faith of these heroes sets them apart from other men. It is your convictions that cause you to be distinctly different from others whose complacency you can't seem to share. The people referred to in Hebrews 11 were not mindful of where they came from. In other words, their minds were full of where they were going. These valiant heroes were not perfect, but they were convinced that what God had promised He was able to perform.

Now if their minds had been full of their origin instead of their destiny, they would have gone back. Be assured that people always move in the direction of their mind. Whatever your mind is full of, that is where you eventually move. Thank God for people who can see the invisible, and touch with their faith the intangible promises of God.

Heroes of Faith

And what more shall I say? For the time would fail me to tell of Gideon and Barak and Samson and Jephthah, also of David and Samuel and the prophets: who through faith subdued kingdoms, worked righteousness, obtained promises, stopped the mouths of lions, quenched the violence of fire, escaped the edge of the sword, out of weakness were made strong, became valiant in battle, turned to flight the armies of the aliens (Hebrews 11:32-34).

The Scriptures declare that these heroes were made strong out of weakness. In order to be a real success, you must be able to be *strengthened through struggle.* What we need is a hero who can, as these men did, report back to the world that he escaped. He may have felt weak, he may have cried and suffered, but he still made it. Look at these men mentioned in Hebrews 11:32.

Examine their lives. They were not glaring examples of flawless character; yet they epitomized faith toward God. Even though most of them experienced failures and flaws, they would have made the front pages of the newspapers in our day for their heroism. We must be careful when judging the weak moments in their lives. Consider the entirety of their lives and you will see that the dent in their armor didn't affect their performance on the battlefield.

Gideon failed the biblical faith test when he sought a sign. Samson shined on the battlefield but had struggles in the bedroom. This anointed judge of Israel wrestled with more than a failed marriage that he could not seem to regain. He had an insatiable appetite for strange flesh, which led to his demise, yet he still made it to the list of the few, the proud, and the brave.

LIFT YOURSELF ABOVE YOUR CIRCUMSTANCES AND FIGHT THE ENEMIES WITHOUT AND WITHIN!

Oh yes, then there is Jephthah, the illegitimate child who was rejected by his siblings and ostracized by his family. He went to the land of Tob where he became what we would call a gang leader. He gathered together the "vain" fellows, a sampling of social rejects, and became their leader. In spite of his adolescent struggles, and his rash tendency to make wild vows (which cost him the destruction of his daughter's future), he still made it to the roll of the renowned. He made it because he believed God. He lifted himself above his circumstances and fought the enemies without and within!

Chosen by Rejection

To me, Jephthah's gang reveals the part of ministry that we are missing: he built an army out of rejects. There is something powerful about being a "chosen reject"; chosen by God but rejected by men. There is a focus that evolves in the heart of someone who has been rejected by men. Their rejection creates a feeling of misplacement. Have you ever felt misplaced? Have you ever struggled to fit into some network or order in which it seemed you were not welcomed? It is God's design that causes us to experience rejection, even though it is painful.

When we have been ostracized by someone or something that we wanted to belong to, our streaming tears cannot soften the hard truth. Rejection tastes like bile in our gut. However, the experience can make us bitter, or it can make us better. I choose better. What about you?

I believe this kind of pain causes us to achieve a level of consecration that is out of the reach of people who have never been rejected. Why? Once the reality hits us that God purposely chooses to use misplaced and rejected people, then first and foremost, we experience a sense of warm gratitude that flows through our human hearts like hot syrup. It fills every crack and crevice of our minds, which suggested there was no place of meaning for us. It is in the shadows of these moments that we worship behind the veil, wrapped in His Shekinah Glory, enveloped in the love of the sacrificed Lamb of God, the God who created a place for the misplaced and chose us for Himself.

I can't help but wonder if we have forsaken some of God's finest people because they were under attack, people whom God wanted to use to make a tremendous statement in the Body of Christ. These vicarious soldiers would have been so glad to receive a second chance to return to active duty. They could bring to us a voice from the grave. They could express the truth that there is life after death.

Fight the good fight of faith, lay hold on eternal life, to which
you were also called and have confessed the good confession
in the presence of many witnesses (1 Timothy 6:12).

Dead circumstances cannot hold down the body of someone who has been chosen! If no one else embraces these bleeding,
purple heart soldiers, perhaps they should rally together and find
comfort in the commonality of their mutual experience. Thank
God for Jephthah, who reminds us of the deep, abiding reality that
even if we were thrown into a refuse receptacle by closed minds
who decided that our dry bones couldn't live again, God is still in
the business of recycling human lives!

GOD IS STILL IN THE BUSINESS OF RECYCLING HUMAN LIVES!

I must confess that more than once I have seen His hand pick
up the pieces of this broken heart and restore back to service my
crushed emotions and murky confidence, while I stood in awe at
the fact that God can do so much with so little. Isn't that the gospel? Isn't that the good news we are supposed to preach to the poor
souls of broken people? Isn't that where the revival must start—in
the trash cans of our churches, in the dumpsters of ministries that
have discarded what God regarded, and regarded what God has
discarded?

The greatest place to preach isn't in our great meetings with
swelling crowds and lofty recognitions. The greatest place to
preach is in the trenches, in the foxholes and the hog pens of life.
If you want a grateful audience, take your message to the messy
places of life and scrape the hog hairs off the prodigal sons of
God, who were locked away in the hog pens by the spiritual elite.

It is here in these abominable situations that you will find true worship being born, springing out of the hearts of men who realize the riches of His grace. No worship seminar is needed for someone whose tear-stained face has turned from humiliation to inspiration. Their personal degradation has become a living demonstration of the depths of the unfathomable love of God! My friend, this is Davidic worship! This is the praise of David, whose critical brothers and distracted father helped him become the canvas on which God paints the finest picture of worship these weary eyes have ever witnessed!

GOD PURPOSELY CHOOSES TO USE MISPLACED AND REJECTED PEOPLE.

I won't even take the time to point out the obvious indiscretions of King David. Even his obvious anointing and worship did not exempt him from internal conflict, or from a lethal experience with infidelity that would have made a heathen blush. No, I don't want to glamorize the sins of these supermen of faith, but I just had to discuss the fact that we have thrown away a hundred others like them. I am afraid we have killed our heroes because we were looking for the brightly packaged, cartoon-clad individuals we read about.

It is time for us to redefine and redirect our gaze to find the heroes of God among us. We must not forget that God purposely chooses to use misplaced and rejected people, and He may be looking in our direction.

Stamina Secrets and Solutions

1. "We need role models and men whose shadows we may stand in, men who provide a cool refreshing place of safety away from the despair of our oppressive society." Do you have a role model? Has your role model ever let you down?

   _____

   _____

   _____

   _____

2. "The whole country has fallen into the trash can like dis-carded comic books whose story lines are out-of-date." Do you agree with this statement? Why or why not?

   _____

   _____

   _____

   _____

3. "Real heroes not only survive the incident, but also over-come the lingering side effects that often come from it." Are you trying your best to *overcome* and *put in the past* the side effects of a painful incident?

   _____

   _____

   _____

4. Whatever your mind is full of, that is where you eventually move. Can you see the invisible and touch with your faith the intangible promises of God?

_____

_____

_____

5. Your personal degradation can become a living demonstration of the depths of the unfathomable love of God! Determine today to be a walking, talking example of God's redeeming love and mercy.

_____

_____

_____

CHAPTER 16

The Only Safe Place

The Word of God calls Noah a *"preacher of righteousness"* (2 Pet. 2:5) who:

> *prepared an ark to the saving of his house; by the which he condemned the world, and became heir of the righteousness which is by faith* (Hebrews 11:7 KJV).

During the 120 years that Noah worked on the ark, he brought his generation God's message of judgment. Over and over again, Noah preached that because of man's wickedness, God was going to send rain so hard and heavy and long that the earth would be deluged with water.

In those days, rain was an unknown phenomenon. The earth, enveloped with a protective canopy, enjoyed a tropical climate year round. Much like a terrarium, the earth's moisture was self-contained, making rain unnecessary.

The people mocked and criticized Noah, calling him a fool for his supposed attempt to save his family and himself from a flood, an idea completely foreign to them. It seemed ludicrous to think that the entire earth could be completely covered with water.

In spite of the ridicule from his peers, Noah preached a controversial, unbelievable, and unpopular message—unlike the widely accepted, lukewarm, and non-confrontational preaching of today. Noah's message was rejected because he preached righteousness in the midst of a wicked and perverse generation. In fact, the only converts he won to God were those of his own household.

What were the days of Noah like? Jesus described them this way:

> *They did eat, they drank, they married wives, they were given in marriage, until the day that* Noah *entered into the ark, and the flood came, and destroyed them all* (Luke 17:27 KJV).

The people acted as if life, as they knew it, would go on forever without interruption. Until the day that Noah entered the ark, the people were neither convinced nor moved by the reality of the impending and inevitable flood. Why were they so skeptical? Because, like the children of Israel in the wilderness, their evil hearts were full of unbelief—and that led to their destruction.

In the end, Noah's persistence, labor, and admonition to his family paid off, and they, along with two of every animal on the face of the earth, were able to escape the doom and destruction of the flood God had promised 120 years before.

After the waters receded, God made a covenant with Noah that He would never again destroy the earth and its inhabitants by way of a flood. Today, when it rains, God places a rainbow in the sky to remind all humankind of His promise to Noah over 5,000 years ago.

The Ark of Safety

God said the next time He destroys the earth because of the wickedness of man, it will not be with water but with fire. Will anyone be safe from God's final judgment of fire?

The only ark and place of safety today is to be baptized by the Spirit of the living God into the Body of Christ, which is represented by the living organism called the Church.

The apostle Paul explained what it means to be *"baptized into one body":*

For by one Spirit we were all baptized into one body— whether Jews or Greeks, whether slaves or free—and have all been made to drink into one Spirit (1 Corinthians 12:13).

There is one body and one Spirit, just as you were called in one hope of your calling; one Lord, one faith, one baptism; one God and Father of all, who is above all, and through all, and in you all (Ephesians 4:4-6).

Local churches function as the arms and legs of the Body of believers, the Church of Jesus Christ.

Some people, however, are reluctant to become members of churches—and for valid reasons. In many cases, churches have failed to meet the spiritual needs of the people.

People come to church hurting, desperate, and needing a touch from God, only to find no comfort, no help, and no word from the Lord. They meet insensitive people who are only concerned about their own needs and feelings and care little about the needs of the lost.

Other seekers briefly find some solace within the sanctum of the four walls of the church. Over the course of time, however, they find themselves taken advantage of and exploited by so-called "church leadership." As a result, they become disillusioned and discouraged from even coming to the house of God.

Then, there are the zealous, new Christians who eagerly desire to serve the Lord, but who, unfortunately, are shunned and hurt by lukewarm church members, jealous of the new members' zeal. Once again, the church fails to meet the needs of those who are looking to them for spiritual guidance and protection.

This, of course, is the plan of the devil, who knows the best way to win a battle is to divide and conquer. If satan can get individual saints isolated and outside the protective covering of a local fellowship of believers, he can convince them they are all alone and nobody cares.

When people are alone—without the help and encouragement of other like-minded believers—they are susceptible to satan's lies. As a result, they begin to think they might as well give up and throw in the towel because, after all, nobody cares anyway.

When people feel isolated, unfortunately, it is often sinners who appear to show more love, concern, and consideration than the hypocritical, pretentious, and condemning saints back at the church. Shame on us.

God's Haven for the Oppressed

As people of God, we must stop simply going through the motions of religious exercises. The reason for assembling together to fellowship and worship is not so we will have a nice place to go or an excuse to show off our latest outfit on Sunday mornings.

The Church is a living entity, a spiritual organism, where abundant life exists here on earth. The Body of Christ must be a present reminder of the hope we have for the hereafter, a place where people can go to escape hell and the wrath to come.

The local church—not Alcoholics Anonymous or the local support group—should be the place where sinners can be freed from their addictions.

God wants to deliver the crack head and the cocaine addict, without admitting them to a substance abuse center—and without withdrawal. The purpose of the local church is to provide a haven where the alcoholic and drug addict can come to Jesus Christ, be set free, and get high on the new wine of the Holy Spirit.

THE LOCAL CHURCH SHOULD BE WHERE SINNERS CAN BE FREED FROM ADDICTIONS.

Homosexuals should not be afraid to come out of the closet and come to church to be delivered by the blood of Jesus and the cleansing power of the Holy Spirit. The church must welcome homosexuals without making them feel they are going to be condemned or persecuted by stiff-necked, two-faced, holier-than-thou, so-called Christians.

If homosexuals, lesbians, fornicators, adulterers, child abusers, molestation victims, rape victims, or rapists can't get set free and delivered in the Church of Almighty God, where else can they be set free? The Church is not a social club; it's a life raft thrown out to the sinking man or woman, boy or girl, who is overcome by sin and dying because of it.

The message of the Church is this: Sinner, you don't have to drown in your sins if you don't want to. God's arm is not too short to reach out and save you. His ears are open to hear your cry for help.

God, in His Word, makes it clear that He is ready and willing to rescue the lost and dying.

> *Behold, the LORD's hand is not shortened, that it cannot save; nor His ear heavy, that it cannot hear* (Isaiah 59:1).

Not only must we convey this message to those who are floundering in their sins, but we need to realize that "rescuing the perishing" is God's purpose for the Church.

Preoccupied Harvesters

Jesus, in discussing the end times with the disciples, said that the coming harvest of souls into the Kingdom of God would signify the end of this present world order.

When asked to explain the parable of the tares (mentioned in a previous chapter), Jesus responded:

> *...the harvest is the end of the world; and the reapers are the angels. As therefore the tares are gathered and burned in the fire; so shall it be in the end of this world* (Matthew 13:39-40 KJV).

Christ's relating of the harvest to the so-called *"end of this world"* has caused some Christians to erroneously assume that the end-time reaping will not take place in our lifetime. As a result, many people in the Church are complacent and insensitive in their desire to see the lost saved.

All around the world, revival is occurring, but some churches seem to be consumed with the "me, myself, and I" attitude. Likewise, we have become lackadaisical in our attempt to live holy lives, ignoring the reality that our Redeemer—as well as our redemption—draws near.

The Body of Christ has become preoccupied with financial prosperity, material well-being, and attempting to satisfy our own spiritual over-indulgence. As a result, we have neglected the work and will of God in evangelizing even those within our own community.

When Jesus was confronted with the same dilemma of choosing between providing for His own personal physical needs or meeting the spiritual needs of others, His response was, *"My food is to do the will of Him who sent Me, and to finish His work"* (John 4:34).

Instead of believing God for the salvation of family, friends, and communities, many are preoccupied with using their faith solely for the purpose of believing God for houses, cars, and vacations. They quote, *"Faith is the substance of things hoped for, the evidence of things not seen"* (Heb. 11:1).

"Things" have come to mean the material and temporal possessions of this world, rather than the eternal "things" of that *"better...heavenly country"* (Heb. 11:16) that the patriarchs of old desired. Instead of setting our affections and sights on things above, realizing that only what we do for Christ will last for eternity, we live contrary to those men and women of faith spoken about in Hebrews chapter 11.

SEEK THE KINGDOM OF GOD FIRST AND ALL OTHER THINGS WILL BE ADDED TO YOU.

This is not to imply that financial and material prosperity is sinful or wrong in and of itself. However, we are admonished to seek the Kingdom of God first and foremost, and inevitably all these other things will be added to us. (See Matthew 6:33.) In fact, we don't necessarily have to believe God for those earthly and material things; they will, without asking, be given to us, as we seek His Kingdom.

Saying "Yes" to God

The harvest is near. In fact, the time has come when the Lord is gathering His people together.

Jesus said that in the last days of earth the householder will gather the children of the Kingdom together. When this happens, the children of God will be vividly distinct from the people of this world. *"Then shall the righteous shine forth as the sun in the kingdom of their Father"* (Matt. 13:43 KJV).

God declares: "I'm gathering My people into the barn. I'm going to put them where the enemy can't get to them. I'm going to put them in a place of safety. I'm going to give them a place of refuge" (see Matt. 13:30).

Regardless of all the violence and destruction presently taking place in this world, God's people are assured of a safe place in the loving hands of Jesus. Speaking of His followers, Jesus said, *"They shall never perish, neither shall anyone snatch them out of My hand"* (John 10:28).

A time comes in every believer's life when he or she decides not to deviate from the straight and narrow path. As a believer, you know you have gone too far with God to turn around and follow the devil. That doesn't mean you won't be tempted to sin or that your trials and tribulations will end.

Serving the Lord is not always easy or popular. Folks may laugh at you on your job, mocking and making fun of your faith. But once you decide that there's no turning back, something in your heart rises up and says "no" to the devil and "yes" to the Lord.

DETERMINE TO PRAISE THE LORD, IN SPITE OF THE CIRCUMSTANCES.

The time comes when you make up your mind that you're going to praise God, even in the midst of the most trying and difficult situations. Drugs are all around, but you will stand firm. Guns are in the streets, but you refuse to be afraid. People robbing, stealing, and killing, but you are determined to praise the Lord, in spite of the circumstances.

As for myself, I must praise Him. Regardless of how rough the road appears to be, I have determined I am going to rejoice and worship and praise the Lord with my whole heart. No matter how strong the battles may rage, with Christ I can do all things; for it is He who strengthens me. (See Philippians 4:13.) Jesus is my place of refuge.

What Is God's Agenda?

If we are seeking God's Kingdom, then we want Him to rule on the earth. The rule of God is His will, and it is not God's will that any should be lost, but that all should be saved. The salvation of the lost is primary on God's agenda.

Is that your top priority in life?

Many in the Church are living only for today rather than storing up treasures for eternity. Our motto has become a hedonistic obsession that says, Live for today, for tomorrow you die.

In Jesus' parable of the rich fool, He wanted to make the point that *"one's life does not consist in the abundance of the things he possesses"* (Luke 12:15).

Americans have taken what Jesus referred to as "abundant life" (see John 10:10) and misinterpreted it as the accumulation of monetary and material wealth. As a result, our attitude has become that of the fool who says, "Chill out, eat, drink, and be merry!"

God's response to this attitude is:

Fool! This night your soul will be required of you; then whose will those things be which you have provided? So is he who lays up treasure for himself, and is not rich toward God (Luke 12:20-21).

According to Deuteronomy 8:18, God has given us power *"to get wealth"* so that His covenant may be established with His people. Salvation, being born again, is the initiation of that covenant relationship.

If we really care about the poor and those less fortunate, we need to get with God's agenda. The best way to help them out of their poverty and despair is to guide them into this covenant relationship with the God of the universe.

DO NOT ALLOW YOUR WEALTH TO BECOME THE FOCUS OF YOUR LIFE.

On the other hand, those of us who have experienced the blessings of God's covenant must not allow our wealth to become the focus of our lives. We must keep our hearts and minds fixed on God's agenda—saving the lost.

Sometimes, however, we get sidetracked. Our attitude about the lost implies that we believe "harvest time" will take place in the far, distant future. As a result, it is not a present reality. Such thinking is contrary to the teaching of Jesus, who said:

> *Do you not say, "There are still four months and then comes the harvest"? Behold, I say to you, lift up your eyes and look at the fields, for they are already white for harvest! And he who reaps receives wages, and gathers fruit for eternal life, that both he who sows and he who reaps may rejoice together* (John 4:35-36).

All the signs of the times indicate, according to the end-time teachings of Jesus, we are near the climax of this present world order and the culmination of biblical prophecies relating to the return of Christ. We should *"walk circumspectly, not as fools,"* but as wise men and women of God, *"redeeming the time"* because the days in which we live are evil and getting worse. *"Therefore do not be unwise, but understand what the will of the Lord is"* (Eph. 5:15-17).

How do you know if you are wise? The Bible says *"he who wins souls is wise"* (Prov. 11:30).

What is the will of the Lord? It is not God's will that anyone be lost, but He wants all people *"to be saved and to come to the knowledge of the truth"* (1 Tim. 2:4).

God's objective is clear. The dilemma presently confronting us—in light of the wickedness in the world—is not that men do not seek to know God. The problem is that the Church has a tremendous shortage of sold-out, unselfish Christians committed to the salvation and discipleship of the lost.

Christian men and women of God must be willing to go into the highways of greed-ridden corporate America and the byways of our sin-ravaged inner cities and compel men, women, and children to come to the Lord.

"...The harvest truly is great, but the laborers are few: therefore pray the Lord of the harvest to send out laborers into His harvest" (Luke 10:2). May that be our most earnest prayer.

Rising to the Occasion

Why is there such an attack on Christians? Why is there so much controversy and slander going on in the organized church, especially now, when the world is in such need of what the true Church of God and His Christ have to offer?

The devil knows that the Church is the most authentic representation of God and His will on earth. Without a spiritually healthy, unified Body of believers, God cannot conduct His affairs on earth in relation to humankind. The devil knows he is no match for God; therefore, in order to wreak his havoc against humankind, he must first try to subdue and defeat the Church, the Body of Christ, in whatever manner and degree he can.

In addition to being a haven for the oppressed, the Church, in many ways, is like a hospital for saints wounded on the battlefield of spiritual warfare. By imparting truth and a fresh anointing of the Holy Spirit, the Church functions as a recuperation center for those who have become weary.

The Church is also a training and assignment base for warriors and ambassadors of Christ. As Jesus' army on earth, the Church upholds the defense against satan and all the works of darkness.

The Bible says that, in these last days, the Church will make known to the principalities and powers in heavenly places *"the manifold wisdom of God...according to the eternal purpose which He accomplished in Christ Jesus our Lord"* (Eph. 3:10-11).

As the Church fulfills her God-ordained purpose here on earth, she will reveal the mystery of God's desire to redeem humankind from the impending destruction that satan hopes to bring upon it. Through the example and leadership of the Church, God seeks to reveal His intent to administer in the affairs of humankind. In essence, the Church on earth is the beginning of *"the kingdoms of this world"* becoming *"the kingdom of our Lord, and of his Christ"* (Rev. 11:15 KJV).

As the pillar of truth, the Church must now rise to the occasion and obey the mandate assigned to her. We must accept the responsibility to be God's battle-ax and weapon of warfare and be used in redeeming this wicked world back to its rightful Lord— Jesus Christ.

Only the Church has the God-given power and right to act and speak to this world on God's behalf. But we must never forget that to whom much is given, much is required. (See Luke 12:48.)

The Church's Finest Hour

We are now quickly approaching the day of the Second Coming of the Lord Jesus Christ. How do we know?

> *Likewise as it was also in the days of Lot: They ate, they drank, they bought, they sold, they planted, they built.... Even so will it be in the day when the Son of Man is revealed* (Luke 17:28,30).

Many preachers are not preparing the Church for the return of Christ. Instead, they are preoccupied with teaching us how to think and grow rich in this world. Rather than inspiring the Body of Christ to win souls to the Kingdom of God and lay up eternal treasures in Heaven, we are taught how to build our own personal kingdoms here on earth.

We need men and women of God who will intercede for the lost souls of our families and communities. We need intercessors who will weep between the altar and the porch of the house of God, so that it will once again become a house of prayer, and no longer a den of wolves and a house of thieves. (See Matthew 21:13.)

The Church desperately needs righteous men and women of God who will lift up their voices like a trumpet and cry aloud. The Church needs *preachers of righteousness* (see 2 Pet. 2:5) who are not afraid to proclaim to the Body of Christ their sins and reveal their transgressions.

A GREAT HARVEST OF SOULS WAITS TO BE WON TO CHRIST.

A great harvest of souls waits to be won to Christ. Men, women, boys, and girls are discouraged and discontent with the world's status quo. They are looking for answers to the problematic and disastrous conditions that plague our society. People are hurting and seeking relief from the pain and heartache of this wicked and perverse generation.

The people of the world are searching for something or someone they can believe in, trust in, and depend on to give them hope and courage to face another tomorrow in this cruel and cold world. As born-again children of God and citizens of the Kingdom of the Lord Jesus Christ, we have the answers to the world's problems, and know the Someone in whom the lost can believe to fulfill every void and save them from the destruction to come.

It is up to us to tell them, *"Whosoever shall call upon the name of the Lord shall be saved"* (Rom. 10:13 KJV).

The apostle Paul asked the Roman Christians:

> *How then shall they call on Him in whom they have not believed? And how shall they believe in Him of whom they have not heard? And how shall they hear without a preacher? And how shall they preach unless they are sent? As it is written; "How beautiful are the feet of those who preach the gospel of peace, who bring glad tidings of good things!"* (Romans 10:14-15)

In this hour, as it was in the days of Noah, we desperately need preachers of righteousness.

Today is harvest time, and the Church must go forth and reap souls for the Kingdom of God.

Other believers have gone before us and planted seeds of righteousness, and many have continued to water the hearts of men with the water of the Word of God. Now it is this generation's responsibility and obligation to go forth and reap the harvest of those who have faithfully labored before us.

This is the Church's finest hour. Although we have a great challenge ahead of us, God has empowered us to successfully complete the assignment. And what an assignment it is!

Stamina Secrets and Solutions

1. "In spite of the ridicule from his peers, Noah preached a con-troversial, unbelievable, and unpopular message—unlike the widely accepted, lukewarm, and non-confrontational preaching of today." Are you ready to receive ridicule from your peers, and even family, as you stand for what you know is God's will for you?

_____

_____

_____

2. If satan can get you isolated and outside the protective cov-ering of a local fellowship of believers, he can convince you that you are all alone and nobody cares. Strength to stand includes being connected with other believers. Are you feeling isolated or are you enjoying the warm fellowship of like-minded believers?

_____

_____

_____

3. The only safe place in Noah's day was on the ark. He preached for years—yet only a few heard—yet he persisted. "The salvation of the lost is primary on God's agenda." Is that your top priority in life?

_____

_____

4. "Rather than inspiring the Body of Christ to win souls to the Kingdom of God and lay up eternal treasures in Heaven, we are taught how to build our own personal kingdoms here on earth." Have you fallen into this trap? It is never too late to turn your focus back on building up God's Kingdom.

_____

_____

_____

5. It is your generation's responsibility and obligation to go forth and reap the harvest of those who have faithfully labored before you. There is strength in numbers. Gather together as many as possible!

_____

_____

_____

CHAPTER 17

Victorious Strength

A mnon was wicked. He brutally raped his sister Tamar. He destroyed her destiny and her future. He slashed her self-esteem. He spoiled her integrity. He broke her femininity like a twig under his feet. He assassinated her character. She went into his room a virgin with a future. When it was over, she was a bleeding, trembling, crying mass of pain.

That is one of the saddest stories in the Bible (see 2 Sam. 13:1-20). It also reveals what people can do to one another if left alone without God. For when Amnon and Tamar were left alone, he assassinated her. The body survived, but her femininity was destroyed. She felt as though she would never be the woman that she would have been had it not happened.

Have you ever had anything happen to you that changed you forever? Somehow, you were like a palm tree and you survived. Yet you knew you would never be the same. Perhaps you have spent every day since then bowed over. You could in no way lift up yourself. You shout. You sing. You skip. But when no one is looking, when the crowd is gone and the lights are out, you are still that trembling, crying, bleeding mass of pain that is abused, bowed, bent backward, and crippled.

HAVE YOU EVER HAD ANYTHING HAPPEN TO YOU THAT CHANGED YOU FOREVER?

Maybe you are in the Church, but you are in trouble. People move all around you, and you laugh, even entertain them. You are fun to be around. But they don't know. You can't seem to talk about what happened in your life.

The Bible says Tamar was in trouble. The worst part about it is, after Amnon had abused her, he didn't even want her. He had messed up her life and spoiled what she was proud of. He assassinated her future and damaged her prospects. Tamar said, "What you're doing to me now is worse than what you did to me at first." She said, "Raping me was horrible, but not wanting me is worse" (see 2 Sam. 13:16).

Maybe you have gone through divorces, tragedies, and adulterous relationships, and you've been left feeling unwanted. You can't shout over that sort of thing. You can't leap over that kind of wall. It injures something about you that changes how you relate to everyone else for the rest of your life. Amnon didn't even want Tamar afterward. She pleaded with him, "Don't throw me away." She was fighting for the last strands of her femininity. Amnon called a servant and said, "Throw her out." The Bible says he hated her with a greater intensity than with which he had loved her before (see 2 Sam. 13:15).

God knows that the Amnon in your life really does not love you. He's out to abuse you. The servant picked up Tamar, opened the door, and threw the victimized woman out. She lay on the ground outside the door with nowhere to go. He told the servant, "Lock the door."

What do you do when you are trapped in a transitory state, neither in nor out? You're left lying at the door, torn up and disturbed, trembling and intimidated. The Bible says she cried. Filled with regrets, pains, nightmare experiences, seemingly unable to find relief...unable to rise above it, she stayed on the ground. She cried.

She had a coat, a cape of many colors. It was a sign of her virginity and of her future. She was going to give it to her husband one day. She ripped it up, meaning, "I have no future. It wasn't just that he took my body. He took my future. He took my esteem and value away."

You may have been physically or emotionally raped and robbed. You survived, but you left a substantial degree of self-esteem in Amnon's bed. Have you lost the road map that directs you back to where you were before?

HAVE YOU LOST THE ROAD MAP THAT DIRECTS YOU BACK TO WHERE YOU WERE BEFORE?

The Lord says, "I want you. I will give you strength for living" No matter how many men like Amnon have told you, "I don't want you," God says, "I want you. I've seen you bent over. I've seen the aftereffects of what happened to you. I've seen you at your worst moment. I still want you." God has not changed His mind. God loves with an everlasting love.

Inner Assurance

Normally, anytime there is a crash, there is an injury. If one person collides with another, they generally damage everything associated with them. In the same way, a crashing relationship affects everyone associated with it, whether it is in a corporate office, a ministry, or a family. That jarring and shaking does varying degrees of damage to everyone involved. Whether we like to admit it or not, we are affected by the actions of others to various degrees. The amount of the effect, though, depends on the nature of the relationship.

What is important is the fact that we don't have to die in the crashes and collisions of life. We must learn to live life with a seat belt in place, even though it is annoying to wear. Similarly, we need spiritual and emotional seat belts as well. We don't need the kind that harness us in and make us live like a mannequin; rather, we need the kind that are invisible, but greatly appreciated in a crash.

Inner assurance is the seat belt that stops you from going through the roof when you are rejected. It is inner assurance that holds you in place. It is the assurance that God is in control and that what He has determined no one can disallow! If He said He was going to bless you, then disregard the mess and believe a God who cannot lie. The rubbish can be cleared and the bruises can be healed. Just be sure that when the smoke clears, you are still standing.

JUST BE SURE THAT WHEN THE SMOKE CLEARS, YOU ARE STILL STANDING.

You are too important to the purpose of God to be destroyed by a situation that is only meant to give you character and direction. No matter how painful, devastated, or disappointed you may feel, you are still here. Praise God, for He will use the cornerstone developed through rejections and failed relationships to perfect what He has prepared!

Lift your voice above the screaming sirens and alarms of men whose hearts have panicked! Lift your eyes above the billowing smoke and spiraling emotions. Pull yourself up—it could have killed you, but it didn't. Announce to yourself, "I am alive. I can laugh. I can cry, and by God's grace, I can survive!"

When Jesus encountered the infirm woman of Luke chapter 13, He called out to her. There may have been many fine women present that day, but the Lord didn't call them forward. He reached around all of them and found that crippled woman in the back. He called forth the wounded, hurting woman with a past. He issued the Spirit's call to those who had their value and self-esteem destroyed by the intrusion of vicious circumstances.

THE HOLY SPIRIT RESTORES THOSE WHO HAD THEIR VALUE AND SELF-ESTEEM DESTROYED BY THE INTRUSION OF VICIOUS CIRCUMSTANCES.

The infirm woman must have thought, "He wants me. He wants me. I'm frayed and torn, but He wants me. I have been through trouble. I have been through this trauma, but He wants me." Perhaps she thought no one would ever want her again, but Jesus wanted her. He had a plan.

She may have known that it would take a while for her life to be completely put back together. She had many things to overcome. She was handicapped. She was probably filled with insecurities. Yet Jesus still called her forth for His touch.

If you can identify with the feelings of this infirm woman, then know that He's waiting on you and that He wants you. He sees your struggling and He knows all about your pain. He knows what happened to you 18 years ago or 10 years ago or even last week. With patience He waits for you, as the father waited for the prodigal son. Jesus says to the hurting and crippled, "I want you enough to wait for you to hobble your way back home."

GOD SEES YOU STRUGGLING AND HE KNOWS ABOUT YOUR PAIN.

When the infirmed woman came to Jesus, He proclaimed her freedom. Now she stands erect for the first time in 18 years. When you come to Jesus, He will cause you to stand in His strength, His anointing. You will know how important you are to Him. *Part of your recovery is to learn how to stand* up and live in the "now" of life instead of the "then" of yesterday.

All you need do is allow His strength and anointing to touch the hurting places. He will take care of the secrets. He touches the places where you've been assassinated. He knows the person you would have been, the person you should have been, the person you could have been. God heals and restores as you call out to Him.

ALLOW HIS POWER AND ANOINTING TO TOUCH THE HURTING PLACES.

The enemy wanted to change your destiny through a series of events, but God will restore you to wholeness as if the events had never happened. He's delivering you by the power of His Spirit—victorious strength.

"Not by might nor by power, but by My Spirit," says the LORD *of hosts* (Zechariah 4:6).

The anointing power of the living God is reaching out to you. He calls you forth to set you free. When you reach out to Him and allow the Holy Spirit to have His way, His anointing is present to deliver you. Demons will tremble. Satan wants to keep you at the door, but never let you enter. He wants to keep you down, but now his power is broken in your life.

I can't help but wonder how much more we all would see of God if we would remove life's little buildups that clog the arteries of our hearts and keep us from seeing the glory of God. These are the obstacles that keep us seeking the wisdom of men rather than the wisdom of God! These are the obstacles that make us feel insecure while we wait for an answer. These are the obstacles that keep many well-meaning Christians needing prayer rather than giving prayer. In short, let's clean out our hearts and we will hear, worship, and experience God in a new dimension. Clean out every thought that hinders the peace and power of God.

Blessed are the pure in heart, for they shall see God (Matthew 5:8).

This Scripture clearly draws a line of prerequisites necessary to see God in His fullest sense. He is often described as the invisible God (see Col. 1:15). God's invisibility doesn't refer to an inability to be seen as much as it does to your inability to behold Him. To the blind all things are invisible. How can I see this God who cannot be detected in my vision's periphery? Jesus taught that a pure heart could see God. No wonder David cried out, *"Create in me a clean heart..."* (Ps. 51:10).

The term used in Matthew 5:8 for pure comes from the Greek word *katharos*, which means to clean out, much like a laxative. That may be funny, but it's true. Jesus is saying to give your heart a laxative when you've heard too much or seen too much. Don't carry around what God wants discarded. Give your heart a laxative and get rid of *"every weight, and the sin which so easily ensnares us"* (Heb. 12:1)! What God wants to unveil to you is worth the cleaning up to see.

Tamar knew the feeling of desertion. She understood that she was cast out. However, the Bible explains that Absalom came and said, "I'm going to take you in." You too may have been lying at the door. Perhaps you didn't have anywhere to go. You may have been half in and half out. You were broken and demented and disturbed. But God sent Absalom to restore you.

THE ANOINTING POWER OF THE LIVING GOD IS REACHING OUT TO SET YOU FREE.

In this instance, Absalom depicts the purpose of real ministry. Thank God for the Church. It's the place where you can come broken and disgusted, and be healed, delivered, and set free in the name of Jesus.

Jesus said:

The Spirit of the LORD is upon Me, because He has anointed Me to preach the gospel to the poor; He has sent Me to heal the brokenhearted, to proclaim liberty to the captives and recovery of sight to the blind, to set at liberty those who are oppressed (Luke 4:18).

You may have thought that you would never rejoice again. God declares that you can have freedom in Him—now! The joy that He brings can be restored to your soul. He identifies with your pain and suffering. He knows what it is like to suffer abuse at the hands of others. Yet He proclaims joy and strength. He will give you the garment of praise instead of the spirit of heaviness (see Isa. 61:3).

Once you have called out to Him, you can lift up your hands in praise. No matter what you have suffered, you can hold up your head. Regardless of who has hurt you, hold up your head!

Lift up your heads, O ye gates; even lift them up, ye everlasting doors; and the King of glory shall come in. Who is this King of glory? The LORD of hosts, He is the King of glory. Selah (Psalm 24:9-10 KJV).

He will restore to you that which the cankerworm and the locust ate up (see Joel 2:25). He said, "I'm going to give it back to you."

Maybe you wrestle with guilt.

"Come now, and let us reason together," says the LORD, "though your sins are like scarlet, they shall be as white as snow; though they are red like crimson, they shall be as wool" (Isaiah 1:18).

All my life I have had a tremendous compassion for hurting people. When other people would put their foot on them, I always tended to have a ministry of mercy. Perhaps it is because I've had my own pain. When you have suffered, it makes you able to relate to other people's pain. The Lord settled me in a ministry that tends to cater to hurting people. Sometimes when I minister, I find myself fighting back tears. Sometimes I can hear the cries of anguished people in the crowd.

Celebrate your victory and thank God you made it!

Like Tamar, you're a survivor. You should celebrate your survival. Instead of agonizing over your tragedies, you should celebrate your victory and thank God you made it. I charge you to step over your adversity and walk into the newness. It is like stepping from a storm into the sunshine—step into it now.

Blessings

God has blessed me with two sons and two daughters. As a father, I have found that I have a ministry of hugs. When something happens, and I really can't fix it, I just hug them. I can't change how other people treated them. I can't change what happened at school. I can't make the teacher like them. I can't take away the insults. But I can hug them!

I believe the best nurses are the ones who have been patients. They have compassion for the victim. The Church needs to develop a ministry of hugs. The touch of the Master sets us free. The touch of a fellow pilgrim lets us know we are not alone in our plight.

The Holy Spirit is calling for the broken, infirm people to come to Jesus. He will restore and deliver. How do we come to Jesus? We come to His Body, the Church. It is in the Church that we can hear the Word of God. The Church gives us strength and nourishment. The Church is to be the place where we share our burdens and allow others to help us with them. The Spirit calls; the burdened need only heed the call.

Three Tenses of Faith

There are three tenses of faith! When Lazarus died, Martha, his sister, said, "Lord, if You would have been here, my brother would not have died." This is *historical* faith. Its view is digressive. Then when Jesus said, "Lazarus will live again," his sister replied, "I know he will live in the resurrection." This is *futuristic* faith. It is progressive. Martha says, "But even *now* You have the power to raise him up again." (See John 11:21-27.)

I feel like Martha.

Even now, after all I—and you—have been through, God has the power to raise us up again! This is the *present tense* of faith. Walk into your newness even now.

You have been anointed with victorious strength!

Stamina Secrets and Solutions

1. Have you had something happen that changed you forever? You knew you would never be the same? *You have the strength to stand* and to become someone even better—through the power of the Holy Spirit. Believe it, say it, live it.

   _____

   _____

   _____

   _____

2. God issues the Spirit's call to all those who have had their value and self-esteem destroyed by the intrusion of vicious circumstances. Open you heart, mind, and soul to the Holy Spirit's comfort and peace.

   _____

   _____

   _____

3. God knows what it is like to suffer abuse at the hands of others. Yet He proclaims joy and strength. You can pro-claim the same joy and strength because of Jesus and His sacrifice especially for you.

   _____

   _____

   _____

4. When you have suffered, it makes you able to relate to other people's pain. How willing are you to help others who are suffering? When you reach out, you will lessen your suffering as well.

_____

_____

_____

5. Even now God has the power to raise you up again. Walk into your newness—now. You are anointed with victorious strength.

_____

_____

_____

About T.D. Jakes

T.D. Jakes is the author of many best-selling books. His weekly morning show, "The Potter's Touch," airs on Trinity Broadcasting and Black Entertainment Television. The Potter's House service streams live every Sunday on www.thepottershouse.org. Bishop Jakes is the founder and pastor of Potter's House, where he ministers to a multicultural congregation of more than 30,000 members.

IN THE RIGHT HANDS, THIS BOOK WILL CHANGE LIVES!

Most of the people who need this message will not be looking for this book. To change their lives, you need to put a copy of this book in their hands.

> *But others (seeds) fell into good ground, and brought forth fruit, some a hundred-fold, some sixty-fold, some thirty-fold* (Matthew 13:8).

Our ministry is constantly seeking methods to find the good ground, the people who need this anointed message to change their lives. Will you help us reach these people?

> *Remember this—a farmer who plants only a few seeds will get a small crop. But the one who plants generously will get a generous crop* (2 Corinthians 9:6).

EXTEND THIS MINISTRY BY SOWING
3 BOOKS, 5 BOOKS, 10 BOOKS, OR MORE TODAY,
AND BECOME A LIFE CHANGER!

Thank you,

Don Nori Sr., Founder
Destiny Image
Since 1982